Phonics, Linguistics, and Reading

PHONICS, LINGUISTICS, and READING

DOLORES DURKIN

University of Illinois

TEACHERS COLLEGE PRESS

Teachers College, Columbia University

New York and London

5/15/78 Beckett Tyler 3 50

PREFACE

In 1958, when I began teaching reading methods courses at the University of California, phonics was getting only skimpy attention in reading methods textbooks. Believing its importance warranted something more, I prepared my own mimeographed material for distribution to students. By the time I left Berkeley two years later, it had been expanded considerably.

Not too long after I joined the Teachers College, Columbia University, faculty, I was asked by the Teachers College Press to write a book dealing with phonics. I did. Called *Phonics and the Teaching of Reading*, it was published in 1962 and reprinted a number of times thanks to many, many people, some of whom were kind enough to write to me about its usefulness.

In 1965 a new edition was published. The most obvious change was the addition of a chapter on linguistics because, by 1965, certain linguists were having an influence on reading that needed to be dealt with.

By the 1970's this influence increased almost to bandwagon proportions. Now there were "linguistic methodologies" for reading, along with many criticisms of some traditional practices. Noticeable, too, was the generous use of linguistic terminology in instructional materials, in particular those for teaching phonics. Thus it seemed time to prepare still another revision. As it happened, probably because the times were different and because I was different, the revision grew into an entirely different book.

Like the original, *Phonics, Linguistics, and Reading* has been written to offer teachers practical help. In addition, its chapters have allowed me to incorporate new learnings and insights, most of which are the product of countless numbers of classroom visits. It is my hope that *Phonics, Linguistics, and Reading* will be able to communicate all this to teachers in a way that will be of assistance as they make and execute plans for teaching phonics.

Dolores Durkin

CONTENTS

Phonics, Linguistics, and Reading

Chapter 1

INTRODUCTION

Phonics instruction is one piece of a total reading program and is given for a single reason: to teach children how to figure out the identity of written words on the basis of their spellings. Or, to put it somewhat differently, phonics helps the child to use letter-sound relationships to identify unfamiliar words. What both of these descriptions indicate is that not all writing systems allow the use of phonics because not all are alphabetic.

WRITING SYSTEMS

Broadly speaking, writing systems are of three kinds. In the order of their historical development they can be described as (a) pictographic, (b) ideographic, and (c) alphabetic.

With pictographic writing, symbols relate directly to the visual appearance of their referents. Thus, a word looks like what it says. According to Bloomfield (1942), "The important feature of picture writing is that it is not based upon language at all. A reader who knows the conventions by which the pictures are drawn, can read the message even if he does not understand the language which the writer speaks" (p. 126). The obvious drawback to pictographic writing is that not all messages are pictureable.

Historically, this led to the development of ideographic writing. With this, each word in a language is assigned a symbol, which shows no rela-

1

tionship to its sound and, generally, none to its meaning, either. Chinese writing is the most perfect system of this kind, although the Japanese—according to at least one author—still use about 1,850 ideographs along with "phonetic letters" (Makita, 1968). The same author also points out that the difficulty of learning to read Japanese ideographic scripts depends upon the extent to which a symbol has changed from the original pictogram—if there was one—to a simplified and conventionalized symbol.

Although it is not ideographic, English does employ ideographs to a limited extent. Examples include mathematical signs ($+$, $=$), numerals (4, 10), and abbreviations (Mrs., Co.). As these few illustrations demonstrate, a reader either knows or doesn't know what an ideograph says. For instance, a reader either knows or doesn't know that 10 stands for the word "ten"; and, if he doesn't know this, there is no way he can figure it out from the ideograph itself. With an alphabetic system this is not so because words are recorded by symbols—letters—that stand for their sounds. Knowing the sounds letters represent can thus be used to learn what word a certain sequence of letters is recording.[1]

English writing is alphabetic. You need not be told that it is not perfectly so, however. If it were, there would be as many letters as there are speech sounds; and, as they recorded words, letters would always stand for the same sounds. As it is, our language has about 42 sounds—the number varies according to whose analysis is used—but only 26 letters to represent them. Unfortunately, all 26 do not make a unique contribution; *c* and *x* and the combination *qu* stand for sounds commonly recorded by other letters. Thus, we have too small an alphabet and, in addition, use it inefficiently. But, who ever said that language is efficient —or logical?

Among other things, the skimpy alphabet means we must expect a letter to stand for more than one speech sound. The letter *a* demonstrates this in words like:

apple   ate   all   art   above

Another difficulty with our writing system is that the same speech sound is sometimes spelled or recorded in different ways. The variety is illustrated by the italicized letters in the following words:

*k*ite   s*ch*ool   pi*ck*   pi*c*nic   bou*qu*et

---

[1] This might be a good time to mention that all languages are "phonetic" because all comprise speech sounds. Only a relatively few, however, use these sounds as the basis for a writing system. When they do, the writing is called "alphabetic" in that letters record the sounds that make up the language.

In addition to these kinds of complications, English also includes words whose sounds are not completely represented in their written symbols:

one   colonel   of

There also are words in which a letter represents no sound, or, as is commonly said, is "silent." For example:

lam*b*   de*b*t   at*e*   co*a*l

Reminders about some of the inconsistencies and even "surprises" characterizing certain words might prompt the conclusion that our language has, indeed, a capricious writing system. Actually, this is not so. As linguists continue to point out, there is much more patterning than is commonly realized (Bloomfield and Barnhart, 1961; Fries, 1963; Hall, 1961). This becomes most apparent, by the way, when the focus is on sequences of letters within a word rather than on an isolated letter. For instance—to take one of the words mentioned earlier—the *b* in lamb *is* "silent" but that is characteristic: When the combination *mb* occurs in the same syllable, it records only the sound that is associated with *m* (*comb, dumb, limb*).

The importance of considering clusters of letters has an implication for phonics instruction. It means that teachers should emphasize not letters in isolation but, rather, letters as they relate to others. Seen from a reader's viewpoint, it means that children should be encouraged to scan the whole of an unknown word before they start making tentative decisions about the sounds individual letters might be representing.

Admittedly, proceeding this way will not always work. In particular, it will not be successful when the unknown word is among the approximately 15 per cent of words in our language whose spellings and pronunciations are anything but a perfect match. A dictionary will quickly show these to be words that are used either very frequently, or only rarely. That some frequently used words *are* irregularly spelled (e.g., *the, was, they*) also bears a message for teaching reading. It means that phonics instruction never is sufficient in and of itself. That is, and right from the start, some words will have to be identified directly for children. (Such identification is traditionally referred to as "whole word methodology.") Thus, even as this book concentrates on phonics, there always is the implicit assumption that some words will be identified rather than analyzed and figured out.

4 ᧘ PHONICS, LINGUISTICS, AND READING

ASSUMPTIONS

Additional assumptions about word identification also are being made. An important one is that the written form of our language frequently offers assistance with word identification through means other than letter-sound relationships. Sometimes contextual cues are available to help. For instance, let us say a child has never seen the written symbol for "pilot." Yet, if it happens to appear in a context such as the following, in which all the other words are known, it is likely that he will be able to read *pilot:*

> He can fly an airplane.
> He is a pilot.

Often, the help that comes from a context lies within a single sentence. Should *hear* be unfamiliar, for example, its identification also would be likely were it found in something like *I can hear the dog bark.*

With both of the contexts cited, the source of help for word identification is the meaning of each. For that reason it would be catalogued as *semantic* help. Closely linked with this is *syntactic* help, in which the construction or grammar of a sentence is the source of productive cues. For example, a sentence like *He is a very tall man* would offer a reader assistance in identifying *very* with the placement of the article *a* and the descriptive word *tall.*

Whether semantic, syntactic, or both, contextual cues are maximally productive for word identification when a reader also is able to take advantage of phonological cues at the same time. Taking advantage of them is what phonics is all about.

OTHER ASSUMPTIONS

Although structural analysis is not the concern of this book, its importance for word identification is recognized. In fact, knowing about word structure (roots, affixes, inflections) is mandatory as written material becomes increasingly more difficult. Even at beginning levels it is important because simple texts can be expected to include plural nouns as well as the various tenses of verbs.[2]

Still another assumption has to do with the relevance of a child's oral language for the successful identification of written words. Illustrating this are the two sentences cited earlier: *He can fly an airplane. He is a*

---

[2] Even though structural analysis is not the concern of this book, it will be discussed in a later chapter to show how phonic and structural analyses work together when a derived or inflected word needs to be figured out by a reader.

pilot. These sentences would be helpful in identifying *pilot* only for the reader who is already familiar with the spoken word "pilot." [3] The ability to use the structure of the sentence *He is a very tall man* to figure out *very* also is dependent upon oral language; and so, too, is the use of phonological cues. Roger Brown (1958) describes the latter dependency very well when he notes:

> The usefulness of being able to sound a new word depends on the state of the reader's speaking vocabulary. If the word that is unfamiliar in printed form is also unfamiliar in spoken form the reader who can sound it out will not understand the word any better than the reader who cannot sound it . . . . the real advantage in being able to sound a word that is unfamiliar in print, only appears when the word is familiar in speech. The child's letter-by-letter pronunciation, put together by spelling recipe, will, with the aid of context, call to mind the spoken form. There will be a click of recognition, pronunciation will smooth out, and meaning will transfer to the printed form. The ability to sound out new words is not simply a pronunciation skill; it is a technique for expanding reading comprehension vocabulary to the size of speaking comprehension vocabulary. This is a considerable help since speaking vocabulary is likely to be ten times the size of reading vocabulary for the primary school child (p. 69).

Brown's reference to "the primary school child" indicates still another assumption of this book. What is to be said is not about the mature reader but, rather, about the child who is still working toward an advanced level of ability. I stress this because every so often an author or speaker criticizes phonics instruction because of the attention it gives to the details of words. The charge is that such a concern is not a realistic reflection of the reading process. More specifically, these individuals claim it fails to recognize that a reader pays little attention to the details of individual words and, in fact, moves along at a rate hardly allowing for a close analysis.

The flaw in such a criticism is its failure to make a distinction between the habits and abilities of an advanced reader, and the needs of the child who is still in the process of learning to read. This book is for those who are helping the latter reach his goal, and concentrates on one of his needs: to figure out the identity of words that are not yet a part of his reading vocabulary. Such identification does require attention to details. Once a word is recognized and learned, however, the need for continued analysis hardly remains. This point needs to be highlighted because classroom observations sometimes reveal the practice of having children

---

[3] Throughout this book, distinctions between spoken and written words will be made by using quotation marks when the reference is to the spoken form of a word and italics when the referent is a written word.

analyze words they are already able to read. Such a procedure turns phonics into an end in itself.

This points to still another assumption: All that is said about phonics in this book views it as a *means* to an end; namely, independence in figuring out unknown words. This role does not reduce the importance of phonics. Rather, the means-end relationship places it in a correct perspective, which, in turn, ought to help teachers recognize the difference between effective and wasteful instruction.

And this prompts a statement of one other assumption of this book, which actually is the reason for writing it. This is the contention that phonics will be effective only when presented by teachers who are thoroughly knowledgeable about it. Consequently, to help those who would profit from knowing more is the goal of this book. To achieve it, the content of phonics is first outlined and discussed. Underlying the coverage is the assumption that teachers must be familiar with all the content before they are ready to select certain parts for certain children.

How to teach selected content is the next concern. Details about this make up Chapter 4. In that chapter attention goes to such basic questions as: When should phonics instruction begin? What are possible teaching procedures? What constitutes a good sequence for instruction?

Recognizing the basic importance of practice for achieving and maintaining skill in word analysis, Chapter 5 includes many examples of ways to have children use what they have been learning. The hope is that the suggestions will help you think of still more possibilities, which seems realistic in that one idea often prompts another.

Before moving to the various components of phonics instruction, it is necessary to discuss the source of a fairly recent influence on phonics, namely, linguistics. This discussion is the theme of Chapter 2.

THE LINGUISTIC INFLUENCE

Linguistics is hardly new. The influence it has had on reading instruction, however, did not develop until the 1960's. The focus of this chapter is the very apparent influence *descriptive linguistics* has had on phonics instruction and phonics materials.

LINGUISTICS

Descriptive, or, as it is sometimes called, structural, linguistics is one of several specializations coming under the broader heading of "linguistics." Its particular concern is for the sign systems of languages. What this means can be explained with a reference to the two subdivisions of descriptive linguistics: phonology and grammar.

Phonology focuses on speech sounds, including their physiological characteristics. It is thus concerned with what linguists call "expression." *Grammar*, the second subdivision, deals with what linguists refer to as "content," and is divided into morphology and syntax. *Morphology* deals with "morphemes," which are the minimal units of meaning in a language. (In English, roots are morphemes but so, too, are affixes and inflectional endings. This means that a word like *do* is one morpheme whereas *undoing* comprises three.) How morphemes are put together to convey meaning goes under the heading of *syntax*.

Another specialization is *historical linguistics*; and, as the name suggests, concentration is on the changes in language over time. Still another

7

specialization in linguistics is *linguistic geography,* which deals with speech variations or dialects within a given language. In the other specialization, *comparative linguistics,* studies are made of the relationships existing among languages of common origin.

To help organize these various subdivisions of linguistics, the following list is presented:

LINGUISTICS
Descriptive Linguistics
Phonology
Grammar
Morphology
Syntax
Historical Linguistics
Linguistic Geography
Comparative Linguistics

As the very brief descriptions of each of these specializations would suggest, it is phonology that has had some influence on phonics.

PHONOLOGY

Phonology is the study or science of speech sounds. According to Hall, "speech sound" is used in definitions "to eliminate grunts, clearings of the throat, screams, and all other possible sounds which do not function as part of the system of human speech" (Hall, 1961, p. 2). Linguists refer to these speech sounds as *phonemes,* a term that is becoming increasingly common in phonics materials.

Phonemes

Phonemes are described in various ways in linguistic literature. Defining them as "significant or functional units of speech sounds" allows for an explanation of the difference between the frequently confused specializations known as phonetics and phonemics (Hall, 1961). *Phonetics* is broad in the sense that it deals with the varieties of speech sounds that occur or can occur in human language. It is concerned with similarities and differences among these sounds, with their articulatory movements, and with the vibrations that account for their acoustic effect. It could thus be defined as the science of describing the sounds of human speech. The International Phonetic Alaphabet, plus still other notations, are used to record them.

Phonemics is more specific and deals with one language at a time. Its aim is to identify the sounds in that language which are significant—that is, are phonemes—in that they account for words which are different in meaning but phonetically the same except for one sound. In English, to cite some examples, the sounds associated with *d* and *t* each constitute a phoneme because they account for words like *dot, tot; dime, time.* In some other language they might not be functional or significant—that is, they might not be separate phonemes—because they do not make for differences in vocabulary.

Still another description of the phoneme allows for an explanation of the term "allophone." I refer here to the one that says a phoneme is "a class of sounds" (Gleason, 1961). Such a definition reflects the fact of variation within one phoneme. For instance, it reflects the linguist's contention that the sounds represented by *k* in words like *key* and *ski* are not identical. And the same would be said about any other phoneme when it appears in different environments.[1] The various subclasses of sounds that compose a phoneme are referred to as *allophones.* With this in mind, a phoneme could be defined as a range of allophones.

Physiological Characteristics of Phonemes

Whatever definition is proposed, all descriptions of phonemes recognize that they differ from one another in those parts of the organs of speech that are involved in their production. Consequently it is not surprising to find that a linguist makes distinctions between the speech sounds which we know as "vowels" and "consonants" in terms of physiological characteristics. For example, one linguist notes:

> We start with the observation that sounds fall into two major types: those in which the stream of air coming from the lungs passes through the mouth and nose with no audible friction, and those in which audible friction is produced. The first category, those produced without audible friction, are called *vowel sounds;* the second, *consonant sounds* (Hall, 1961, p. 7).

Another observes:

> We know that consonants result when, in speaking, the outgoing breath stream is either partially or completely obstructed by the organs of speech. Vowels result when the organs of speech merely modify the resonance chamber without impeding the flow of outgoing breath (Cordts, 1965, p. 138).

Those not trained in phonetics need to keep in mind this stress on physiological characteristics because many of the distinctions linguists make among speech sounds are based not so much on what is heard as on what is required to produce them. This accounts for their "semivowel" description of the sounds recorded by *y* in *yes* and by *w* in *we.* In phonics, those are classified as consonant sounds to distinguish them

---

[1] "Environment" refers to the placement of a phoneme; that is, to its position in a syllable and thus to the other phonemes that precede and/or follow it.

from the way *y* and *w* function in words like *try, myth, carry, owl, raw,* and *few*. Linguists, on the other hand, say the initial sounds in *yes* and *we* are semi-vowels because they "are like the vowels in the positions in which they are pronounced, but like the consonants in that they are pronounced with audible friction" (Hall, 1961, p. 9).

Other linguistic descriptions of speech sounds also reflect attention to physiological characteristics. Only those appearing in phonics materials will get attention.

Phonetic Descriptions of Phonemes

For the phonetician, a single speech sound is the product of one set of adjustments of the organs of speech. More than one adjustment results in more than one sound. According to this definition the sound recorded by *t* in *tam* is a single sound, but what *j* records in *jam* is a blend of two sounds. (Remember: what you think you hear is less important for phonetic classifications than is the speech mechanism involved in the production of the sound.) Following the same definition, the sound that *sh* represents in *ship* is a single sound, whereas what *ch* represents in *chip* is a blend of two. It can thus be seen that single sounds are represented by either one or more than one letter and, secondly, that blends of sounds are also represented by both single letters and combinations.[2]

One combination of sounds dealt with by both the reading teacher and the phonetician is the *diphthong,* which is a blend of vowel sounds— or, to be more precise, a blend of vowel and semi-vowel sounds. Ordinarily, the reading teacher only considers the diphthongs that are recorded with two letters; but, as the following list shows, some are spelled with a single letter:

oil   owl   ice
boy   out   use

When certain sounds recorded by *a, e,* and *o* are prolonged as they are in, respectively, *may, he,* and *so,* they, too, are classified as diphthongs by some linguists. Others, however, describe them as single sounds (Gleason, 1961).

In phonics instruction, the sounds represented by *a, e, i, o,* and *u* and heard in initial position in, respectively, *ate, eat, ice, old* and *use* have been traditionally referred to as the "long" vowel sounds. What the same letters record in, respectively, *at, end, if, on,* and *us* have been described as the "short" sounds. Most phonics materials continue to use

---

[2] Actually, the phonetician's concern is not for the way sounds are spelled; this is in contrast to the reading teacher's concern and accounts for some of the confusions when linguistists and reading specialists try to talk to one another.

these descriptions, although one set of materials now employs the terms "glided" (long) and "unglided" (short). Hall (1961) offers the physiological explanation for these terms:

> In some vowel sounds it makes a difference whether the tongue muscle is tense (as in the vowel sound of *beat*) or lax (as in the vowel sound of *bit*); normally this tenseness is accompanied by a gliding movement of the tongue upward, whereas the lax vowels do not have such an upward tongue-glide (p. 7).

Because just about all phonics materials continue to use the terms "long" and "short" when they refer to ten of the vowel sounds, this book will also use them. It should still be pointed out nonetheless that phoneticians employ "long" and "short" differently and, in fact, in a literal fashion. That is, they use these descriptions to refer to the extent to which a vowel sound is prolonged in a word. They would say, for instance, that the sound recorded by *e* in *bet* is shorter in duration than what it represents when appearing in a word such as *bed*. Or, to cite another illustration, they would note that the sound recorded by *e* in *beat* takes less time to pronounce than the sound recorded by *i* in *bid*.

What affects the duration of vowel sounds in words are the sounds that follow them: "Before a final voiced consonant, vowel sounds are lengthened" (Prator, 1958). Although the phonetic description "voiced" is not common in phonics materials, it—along with "voiceless"—will be dealt with here because in a later chapter these terms enter into the discussion of a sequence for teaching phonics.

Prator's *Manual of American English Pronunciation* (1958) contains this explanation of voiced and voiceless sounds:

> An important way in which one speech sound may differ from another is in voicing or the lack of it. We say that a sound is *voiced* if *our vocal cords vibrate* as we pronounce it; a sound is *voiceless* if it is pronounced *without such vibration* (p. 63).

All vowel sounds are voiced. Consonant sounds, on the other hand, divide between some that are voiced and some that are voiceless. Certain phonetic pairings of the two kinds of consonant sounds have relevance for phonics instruction; they are listed below:

Voiced Consonants	Voiceless Consonants
/b/	/p/
/d/	/t/
/g/	/k/
/v/	/f/
/z/	/s/

That the sounds in each of the above pairs are similar is what assigns relevance to the classifications "voiced" and "voiceless" insofar as phonics instruction is concerned. More will be said about them when the sequence of that instruction is discussed in Chapter 4.

Because the phonetic classification "stop" also has relevance for phonics, that, too, needs to be explained. Again, a brief passage from Prator's *Manual* (1958) is helpful:

> It is sometimes useful to classify consonants as *stops* or *continuants*. A continuant is a sound—like [m]—which may be prolonged as long as the speaker has breath to pronounce it. A stop must be pronounced instantaneously, and cannot be held—like [t] (p. 64).

Six consonant sounds are classified as "stops":

$$/b/ \quad /p/ \quad /d/ \quad /t/ \quad /g/ \quad /k/$$

Because of the nature of these six sounds, attempts to pronounce them apart from words in which they appear lead to noticeably distorted pronunciations (e.g., "buh," "puh"). This is what makes the classification "stop" pertinent for those who are teaching phonics, and is the reason why it will be referred to again in a subsequent chapter.

Method for Identifying Phonemes

As the previous section has shown, the phonemes of a language are identified and classified with a reference to their physiological characteristics. (Only a few of those characteristics were mentioned because only a few have direct relevance for phonics.) Another way to consider the identification of phonemes is through what linguists call the "method of contrast." This must be mentioned because it has influenced some of the more recent proposals and materials for teaching phonics.

To introduce this discussion of the method of contrast, it might be helpful to repeat what was said earlier about the goal of phonemics: "to identify the sounds in a language that are significant—that is, are phonemes—in that they account for words which are different in meaning but phonetically the same except for one sound." It was also said that, "In English, to cite some examples, the sounds associated with *d* and *t* each constitute a phoneme because they account for words like *dot, tot; dime, time.* In some other language they might not be functional or significant—that is, they might not be separate phonemes—because they do not make for differences in vocabulary."

The material just quoted offers indirect information about the identification of phonemes through the method of contrast. A passage from Gleason's (1961) very helpful text, *Descriptive Linguistics,* is more explicit:

To find the phonemes we must compare samples of spoken English that are distinct both in expression and content . . . . *Bill* (a man's name) and *bill* (a request for payment) are obviously different in content. But they are not recognizably different in expression . . . . Such a pair is of no use in determining the phonemes of English . . . .
If the two samples are *bill* and *pill*, there is both a difference of content and a difference of expression . . . . Irrespective of the context or lack of it, an American can distinguish these two words as they are said by any native speaker. The two must therefore differ in at least one significant feature in the expression system, that is, in at least one phoneme . . . . We find that *bill* and *pill* differ in only one phoneme. They are therefore a *minimal pair* (pp. 15–16).

Brought out in this brief description is the meaning of "method of contrast" and, too, of "minimal pair." Later in the chapter it will be shown how the use of both now appears in phonics materials. First, though, we need to introduce into this discussion still other linguistic terms; to do this, attention must shift from spoken to written English.

WRITTEN ENGLISH

As was mentioned in Chapter 1, the visual representation of our language is related to its sounds. That is, English has an alphabetic writing system in which letters are used to stand for sounds. Also mentioned was that single letters represent both single sounds and blends; the same is true of certain pairs of letters, sometimes referred to as *digraphs*.

Linguists call the letters of an alphabet *graphemes*. Consequently it could be said that just as the phoneme is the basic unit of spoken language, so the grapheme is the basic unit of written language.[3]

For the linguist, written language is a *code*. This accounts for still another new term in phonics materials: *decoding*. It is now used to refer to the process of figuring out the identity of written words on the basis of letter-sound relationships. Or, to use still more of the new terminology, decoding is the process of identifying written words on the basis of *grapheme-phoneme correspondences*.

To highlight distinctions between graphemes and phonemes, linguists use symbols enclosed in diagonal lines when the reference is to the latter. Thus, *b* is a grapheme whereas /b/ refers to a phoneme; specifically, to the phoneme that *b* stands for in words like *but* and *cab*.

For almost all the consonant sounds, the symbol enclosed in the slash marks is identical to the grapheme associated with it. (This was just

---

[3] The term "grapheme" is not confined to the letters of an alphabet. Chinese characters, for instance, are not letters, but they are still referred to as graphemes.

illustrated with *b.*) For vowel sounds and for blends, the symbol commonly is different, as the following samples illustrate:

orthographic symbol	phonetic symbol	as in
o	/a/	on
i	/ay/	ice
u	/ə/	up
a	/e/	ate
	/ey/	
sh	/š/	shut
	/ʃ/	
ch	/č/	chop
	/tʃ/	
j	/ǰ/	jam
	/dʒ/	

Even with these few samples, certain points about phonetic notations can be made. For instance, /a/ and /ay/ demonstrate how notations indicate physiological similarities among sounds; in this case, similarity in the sounds known in phonics as the short sound of *o* and the long sound of *i*. (The phonetic symbol for the latter also shows that it is a diphthong; that is, a close blend of a vowel sound and a semi-vowel sound.) Also suggested is the lack of agreement among linguists when it comes to transcribing or symbolizing certain of the phonemes. And being suggested, too, is still another term that now appears in phonics materials; namely, *orthography*, which refers to written language. Using this term, it could be said that phonics instruction makes use of the relationship between orthography and phonology to help children identify written words.

LINGUISTS' CRITICISMS OF PHONICS INSTRUCTION

Now that some of the terms and methods of study employed by linguists have been mentioned, it seems timely to introduce into the discussion the so-called "linguistic criticisms" that have been leveled at phonics instruction in recent years. In doing this, what must be emphasized immediately is that very few linguists have been involved. In fact, it seems safe to say that, if queried, the vast majority of linguists would quickly admit to knowing nothing about reading instruction, including phonics. Nonetheless, a few have been openly and even sharply critical—notably, Bloomfield (Bloomfield and Barnhart, 1961) and Fries (Fries, 1963).

Also in need of quick emphasis is that not all among the critics are true linguists in the sense that not all have been extensively trained in the various specializations coming under the heading of linguistics. Some, for example, have academic backgrounds in English; others are professional educators who have taken some courses in linguistics. The points being emphasized, then, are two: (a) The criticisms directed at phonics instruction have come from relatively few individuals, and (b) among the few, not all are linguists.

Early Criticisms

Although widely known now, the earliest of the linguistic criticisms won little attention when they appeared in a 1942 article in *Elementary English Review* (Bloomfield, 1942). At that time the critic was Leonard Bloomfield, a highly regarded linguist. Although his criticisms might seem old, they will still be described because they are very much like the seemingly unending complaints that suddenly blossomed in the 1960's.

One of Bloomfield's first complaints was leveled not at phonics but at the school's use of whole word methodology to develop reading vocabularies. (This procedure directly identifies entire words for children.) Bloomfield said that such a method ignored the alphabetic nature of our writing system and, in fact, treated it as if it were ideographic.

Another of his complaints—and this is very typical of what was to be heard later in the 1960's—focused on the kinds of words being selected for beginning reading materials. Bloomfield argued that far too many had irregular spellings; these would include such words as *was* and *they* and also *come, guess,* and *said.* He also pointed out that some of the letters composing other more regularly spelled words stood for more than one sound. Opposed to this, he offered an alternative:

> Our first reading material must show each letter in only one phonetic value; thus, if we have words with g in the value that it has in *get, got, gun,* our first material must not contain words like *gem,* where the same letter has a different value . . . . Our first material should contain no words with silent letters (such as *knit* or *gnat*) and none with double letters, either in the value of single sounds (as in *add, bell*) or in special values (as in *see, too*), and none with combinations of letters having a special value (as *th* in *thin* or *ea* in *bean*) . . . . No matter how well we plan in other respects, our teaching will yield inferior results so long as the material which we present is clumsily chosen (Bloomfield, 1942, pp. 185–186).

Although most of the linguist-critics [4] echo this same general plea

---

[4] The term "linguist-critic" will be used to refer to those who have based their criticisms on certain assumptions and ways of proceeding that characterize linguistics. It thus includes individuals who are not linguists.

for phonetic consistency and regularly spelled words in beginning materials, their detailed proposals are not always similar. Noteworthy here are the recommendations found in Bloomfield's *Let's Read* (Bloomfield and Barnhart, 1961) and in Fries' *Linguistics and Reading* (1963). Interestingly, words classified as "regular" by one of these linguists are called "irregular" by the other.

Isolation of Phonemes

This emphasis on phonetic consistency and spelling patterns, coupled with the criticism of whole word methodology, makes it seem logical to conclude that the linguist-critic would applaud phonics instruction. In fact, though, that hardly has been the case. Some of the sharpest criticisms—and they had their beginnings in the 1942 article by Bloomfield —have been aimed directly at certain features of certain types of phonics. In particular, they have been directed toward the practice of isolating phonemes from words. (E.g., "What sound does *d* stand for in *doll* and *day?*") These same critics have also accused phonics teachers of acting as if they are teaching a child to speak rather than to read when they have him synthesize phonemes (a→ac→act) in order to decode written words.

Both of these criticisms reflect the linguist's contention that phonemes have no existence outside words. Instead, it is emphasized, they are abstractions that find their realization in words (Fries, 1963). Within such a framework, attempts to pronounce isolated phonemes are viewed as a process which distorts them to such a degree that the resulting sounds no longer are the phonemes in question. Linguists would also maintain that the same process fails to recognize that every phoneme is a class or range of allophones and is thus realized differently in different environments.

Incorrect Terminology

Along with the criticism of phoneme isolation comes still more; for instance, criticism of the language used in connection with phonics instruction. To describe this complaint, expressions that some reading teachers might use will appear below in italics. Following each, a reaction will appear as it might be given by a linguist-critic. Following that, I offer my own reaction.

You can hear the sound of "f" at the beginning of words like "fall" and "first."

LINGUIST-CRITIC'S REACTION: Letters do not have sounds; they simply record or represent them. Consequently it is incorrect to refer to "the sound of *f*."

My Reaction: I doubt that any teacher thinks that letters have sounds in the sense that I now have a pencil in my hand. An expression like "the sound of *f*" is simply less cumbersome than others such as "the sound that *f* represents" or "the sound that *f* stands for." Ease of expression, I would like to suggest, also is the reason why some of the linguist-critics themselves slip into language like "the sound of *f*" and why, in addition, the same will be found in this book.

What sound do you see at the end of "plant"?

Linguist-Critic's Reaction: Sounds are not seen, they are heard.
My Reaction: Nobody can quarrel with this.

Pairs of letters like "bl," "st," and "dr" are called "consonant blends."

Linguist-Critic's Reaction: It is combinations of sounds that are blends, not combinations of letters.
My Reaction: This is another example of a valid criticism. Acceptance of it is reflected in the more recent phonics materials in which letter combinations like *bl*, *st*, and *dr* are referred to as "clusters," whereas the sounds they record are called "blends."

The following are diphthongs: oy, oi, ow, ou, ew.

Linguist-Critic's Reaction: The term "diphthong" refers to sounds, not letters.
My Reaction: Again, this is a valid criticism, for it has been common in phonics instruction to confuse the term "diphthong" and "digraph." Diphthongs, as has been pointed out before, are blends of vowel and semi-vowel sounds. A digraph, on the other hand, is a pair of letters.

The best way to summarize all these comments about the language of phonics instruction is to say that it sometimes fails to make distinctions between statements about sounds and statements about the letters used to record them. When this happens, criticism is justified.

LINGUISTIC PROPOSALS FOR READING

Along with the linguists' criticisms have come their proposals for teaching beginning reading. (The well-known and influential proposals have not been concerned with the advanced reader.) Some of these recommendations have already been mentioned at least indirectly. All will now be described in a little more detail.

Selection of the Beginning Vocabulary

As was brought out earlier, the linguist-critics have urged that the selection of vocabulary for beginning materials be based on spelling patterns. Were one to follow this recommendation, words from a single pattern would be taught first. For example, were the consonant-vowel-consonant pattern selected for initial attention, choices might include words like *fat, cat,* and *hat.* Gradually, other words from the same pattern would be introduced—perhaps *hit, fan, cup, pet,* and so on.

Once a collection of words from a given pattern was learned, the beginning reader would then be introduced to others from a different pattern. If the next one was the consonant-vowel-consonant-final *e* pattern, choices could include such words as *made, cute, like,* and *rode.* If it were the consonant-vowel-vowel-consonant pattern, words like *meat, road,* and *mail* would be appropriate.

For those who might not be too familiar with reading instruction, it should be noted that prior to the arrival of the linguist-critic, three other criteria were commonly used for selecting words. The criterion of usefulness—one that linguists still must attend to—accounted for the appearance of words like *the* and *what* in beginning materials. The other criteria of meaningfulness and interest could result in the selection of words like *play, mother,* and *ball.*

Method of Teaching Selected Vocabulary

In addition to offering advice about selecting vocabulary, the linguist-critics have been proposing a method for teaching it that is closely linked to spelling patterns. It involves both "minimal pairs" and the "method of contrast," terms that are defined below:

> *Minimal Pair*—Two words that differ by only one phoneme; for example, *make* and *take, hat* and *had.*
>
> *Method of Contrast*—A way of identifying phonemes by comparing and contrasting minimal pairs.

The method of contrast, used in reading instruction, would have teachers present new vocabulary in contrast with familiar words. The new and the familiar would always constitute a minimal pair. Both words could be from the same pattern; for instance, *fat* might be presented with the known word *cat.* Or, two contrasting patterns might be used, in which case something like *cap* might be presented in contrast with *cape.*[5]

Quotes from Bloomfield's *Let's Read* (Bloomfield and Barnhart, 1961) and from Fries' *Linguistics and Reading* (1963) further explain the "linguistic" way of teaching vocabulary, and also indicate how it is essentially different from phonics. For example, Bloomfield (Bloomfield and Barnhart, 1961) has said:

---

[5] No attempt will be made here to describe in full this use of the method of contrast and minimal pairs. For those interested, manuals for the so-called "Linguistic Readers" provide all the necessary details (Fries, Wilson, and Rudolph, 1966; Rasmussen and Goldberg, 1970; Smith *et al.,* 1965).

When we present a pair of words like *can* and *fan*, a child may have no notion that these words are similar in sound, or that the similar spelling indicates a similar sound. It would be a waste of time to try, as do the advocates of "phonic" methods, to explain this to him. All we do is present such words together; the resemblance of sound and spelling will do its work without any explanation from us (p. 42).

In *Linguistics and Reading*, Fries says:

At the beginning and for considerable time thereafter the teacher pronounces in *normal talking fashion* each new word and each pair of contrastive words as it is introduced and makes sure that the pupil, from that pronunciation, identifies the words as ones he knows.

Only complete words are pronounced. The pronunciation for the "word" is thus attached to the total spelling-pattern that represents that word . . . . Sounds are not given to the separate letters of a spelling-pattern. The understanding of the difference that any particular letter makes in the spelling-pattern is built up out of the experience of pronouncing a variety of word pairs with minimum differences in their *spelling-patterns*.

CAT——AT
CAT——RAT
CAT——PAT

We avoid completely such a question as "What does the letter C say?" (pp. 203–204).

In a passage in Bloomfield's book, another contrast is made with phonics:

In most of the words . . . the letter *a* is followed by a single consonant letter, and this, in turn, by a silent *e*, as in *cake, cape, game, safe* . . . . Some other words of the present section have the letter *a* followed by a single consonant letter which in turn is followed by *le*, as in *table, cradle*. Others have *a* followed by a single consonant letter with suffixal *y* after it, as *lady, gravy*. In short, we could state some rules about English spelling which would cover these words . . . . To be sure, these rules would be rather complicated. We shall not try to explain such things to the child (Bloomfield and Barnhart, 1961, p. 284).

Combined, the three quoted passages underscore key elements in the methodology proposed by the linguist-critics. One, clearly, is the avoidance of direct explanations of letter-sound relationships. Instead, understanding "the difference that any particular letter makes"—to use Fries' words—is to come from experiences with minimal pairs. For example, to be induced from the experience of learning to read words like *fan* and *man* and, perhaps, *fit* and *sit* is an understanding of the difference that f makes. It goes without saying that another key element is the avoidance of attempts to isolate and explicitly identify phonemes—for instance, the one that f stands for in *fan* and *fit*.

One other key element is the use of spelling patterns to select vocabulary. Further, when words are taught they are spelled but, once again, no direct explanation is given of the relationship between a pattern and a pronunciation. Unlike phonics, for example, attention is *not* given to such generalizations as: A single vowel in a closed syllable usually records its short sound.

As a quick summary it could be said that the methodology proposed by the linguist-critics is one that does everything to avoid isolating phonemes from the words in which they appear.

Other Proposals for Reading

Although the proposals just described have won most of the reading specialists' attention, still others have been made by certain of the linguist-critics. Some, for instance, have proposed that pictures be omitted from beginning readers—a suggestion that stands in great contrast to what can be found in the vast majority of easy textbooks now available. One reason given for such a suggestion is that pictures are distracting to the reading process. Another is the temptation for children to use the content of a picture rather than the spelling of a word as a prompt for its identification. More specifically, if a child fails to recognize *toys*, he might seek help in a picture showing a little boy playing with some balls instead of in the letters composing *toys*. (Unfortunately, some teachers foster just such a temptation.) This practice, certain linguist-critics point out, can lead not only to incorrect identification (*toys* read as "balls") but also to the undesirable habit of relying on pictures rather than spellings when unfamiliar words are met. Authors of some of the so-called "linguistic readers" have heeded this particular warning by either omitting illustrations entirely or by including only pictures and decorations that have little or no direct connection with a text's content.

Since linguists, by the very nature of their specialization, are primarily concerned with spoken language, it is not at all surprising that some of the critics have also been pushing for increased amounts of oral rather than silent reading. Because most primary-grade teachers conduct programs in which oral reading predominates, this particular proposal has had little noticeable effect on instructional practices.

REACTION TO PROPOSALS AND CRITICISMS

The linguistic readers now available (Fries, Wilson, and Rudolph, 1966; Rasmussen and Goldberg, 1970; Smith *et al.*, 1965) embody most of the suggestions that have been coming from the linguist-critics during the past decade; consequently they have been providing researchers with the opportunity to assess their value. Unfortunately, though, such opportunity has not been used in a way or to an extent that would allow for reliable, objective assessments. That is, reported studies have been few and, among the few, high quality work is not always characteristic. My own visits to classrooms have also uncovered a problem not always taken into account by researchers: Some teachers use linguistic readers in a way that is essentially different from what was envisioned by their authors.

Lacking empirical evidence, I am now only able to state some opinions regarding the various proposals that have been made by the linguist-critics. Because of the concern of this book, they will be confined to those that have some bearing on phonics instruction. The proposals that are unrelated have been dealt with elsewhere (Durkin, 1970; Durkin, 1972).

Terminology

One frequent proposal made by the critics has to do with the need to use more linguistically correct terminology in phonics instruction. Although this appears to be a very reasonable and valid proposal, it nonetheless must be examined before it is wholeheartedly accepted and put into practice.

What has to be considered immediately, for instance, is the goal of phonetics in contrast with the goal of phonics. In phonetics, the aim is precisely accurate descriptions of speech sounds. Going along with this aim has been the necessary development of a highly technical vocabulary, which sometimes refers to distinctions that would be discernible only to persons trained in phonetics.

In contrast, the aim of phonics is a pragmatic one: to help children use letter-sound relationships to figure out the identity of written words. With this as its goal, whatever works—that is, whatever helps children become successful decoders—is "good" phonics instruction. Obviously, if good instruction also makes use of technically correct terminology, so much the better. Yet, at no time should the terminology become an end in itself. With the aid of some illustrations, let me explain what I mean.

Because of their physiological characteristics, the sounds recorded by *y* and *w* in, respectively, *yes* and *want* are categorized as "semi-vowels" by phoneticians. In phonics, on the other hand, they have been traditionally referred to as consonant sounds to distinguish them from the vowel sounds that *y* and *w* represent in such words as *try*, *gym*, *owl*, and *law*. Because the "semi-vowel" classification relates to certain characteristics of speech sounds that are not obviously apparent to children and, further, because such terminology is not likely to increase a child's decoding skills, there seems to be no need to change to the phonetician's classification, even though from a scholarly point of view it is correct.

The sound—or I should say sounds—recorded by *j* can serve as another illustration of why one does not always have to act like a phonetician when teaching phonics—maybe, even, why one *should* not. As was mentioned before, according to the phonetician's classification *j* records a blend of two sounds in words like *jam* and *jump*. Again, however, this reflects changes in speech mechanisms that would not be apparent to children. Too, such a classification is not likely to improve phonics instruction when improvement is viewed in the context of its central, practical goal. For these two reasons, *j* will continue to be described in this book as recording a single consonant sound in words like *jam* and *jump*.

One change that will be noted is the use of such linguistic vocabulary as "phoneme" and "grapheme." To be underscored immediately is that the inclusion of these and other linguistic terms is not based on any conviction that they are all essential, or on any expectation that they will automatically improve phonics instruction. Rather, they are used in subsequent chapters because they appear in current instructional materials; thus teachers need to learn to feel comfortable with them. This seems reason enough to employ such terms in this book.

Other terms are used and other distinctions are made because they represent corrections suggested by the linguist-critics that cannot be ignored. To cite some examples, "blend" will be used to refer to sounds whereas "cluster" will be reserved for letters. Similarly, "diphthong" will refer to a certain type of sound whereas the referent for "digraph" will always be letters. Even with these terms, not all the distinctions made by the phonetician will be made in this book. For instance, what *bl* records in *blue* will be considered a blend—which is what the phonetician would say and is what a child could hear. However, because children in the process of becoming mature readers are not always able to hear each of the two sounds recorded by *oi* (oil), *oy* (boy), *ow* (owl), *ou* (out), *i* (ice), and *u* (use), diphthongs will be treated in this book as if they were single sounds, even though the phonetician classifies them as blends.

In summary, every effort has been made to use correct terminology. Yet at no time is terminology treated as an end in itself, nor has any special effort ever been made to try to appear up-to-date by sprinkling linguistic terminology here and there. Instead, the single aim is to present a practical book that will help teachers become maximally effective in teaching phonics and thus maximally successful in getting children to use letter-sound relationships to figure out the identity of written words.

Selection of Vocabulary

In addition to underscoring the need for more precisely correct terminology, the linguist-critics have also been saying, and almost in unison, that words ought to be selected for beginning materials on the basis of spelling patterns and phonetic consistency. What is the value of such suggestions?

As was mentioned before, whether the use of these combined criteria will lead to increased reading achievement still awaits empirical verification. Meanwhile, it is only possible to make observations about the materials that have resulted when these particular criteria were used (Fries, Wilson, and Rudolph, 1966; Rasmussen and Goldberg, 1970; Smith *et al.*, 1965).

Certainly one thing the materials demonstrate is that more interesting content is not guaranteed when the newly proposed criteria are employed. Something like *Dan can fan*, for example, hardly seems superior to what resulted when the more traditional vocabulary selection was tightly controlled, thus making unnatural repetition a necessity (*Oh, oh, oh. Look, look, look.*). The "linguistic" materials also demonstrate that the task of writing sentences—even the simple, unexciting kind—quickly requires the use of words whose pronunciations, in relation to their spellings, fail to fit into any pattern (*the, was, they*). Thus they point to the impossibility of adhering strictly to the combined criteria proposed by the linguist-critics. Still, the move by some toward an early and extensive use of patterned words is something meriting serious study; in particular, study of its effect on a child's eventual achievement in reading. Until such research is done, what is being proposed will remain simply the educated guess of some linguists.

Method of Teaching Vocabulary

As was pointed out earlier, the methodology offered by the linguist-critics assumes phonetic consistency and contrast to be the factors that allow children to learn to read new words quickly. This is why the concentration is on minimal pairs; for example, on words like *bat* and *fat*, *bun* and *fun*, and so on. It must be noted that two other assumptions also are made. One is that the stress on minimal pairs will instruct a child—without any explanations from teachers—about the differences that letters make to words; for instance, the differences that *b* and *f* make. The other taken-for-granted assumption is that knowing about these differences has automatic transfer value. That is, it enables a child to identify words not formally taught. Thus, if he has been taught *ball*, it is assumed that earlier instruction with other minimal pairs means he will automatically know what *fall* says. To sum up, (a) rapid learning,

(b) inductive learning, and (c) transfer of learning are all assumed. Can they be?

My own teaching experience, combined with frequent visits to classrooms, prompts me to ask, "But where is your evidence?" Evidence seems essential because, for example, although patterned material *might* foster more rapid learning than has been typical, it also requires more practice than is typical. In fact, and in fairness to the linguist-critics, it must be said that they admit that their proposed methodology requires large amounts of practice (Bloomfield and Barnhart, 1961; Fries, 1963). What they fail to offer, however, are suggestions for carrying it on with young children in a way that will avoid their developing negative attitudes toward reading. For that reason it must be asked whether a method that requires what some would consider to be excessive amounts of practice is a suitable one for younger children. Henry Lee Smith (1963), himself a linguist, has also observed that his own experiences with patterned material indicate that "rapid learning" is not as common as has been suggested by the linguist-critics. He comments that "their suggestions seem to be based on the educated guesses of a linguist, not on research or experiences with average children" (p. 77).

The same comment could be directed to the other assumption made by the linguist-critics; namely, that both inductive learning and transfer take place automatically. Contrary to that, classroom observations continually uncover children for whom neither inductive learning nor its transfer to other situations is automatic or even easy. What this suggests is the need to research the validity of what is being assumed about so-called "linguistic" methodology and, secondly, to research it with subjects who vary in such relevant factors as intelligence. It certainly is in the realm of possibility that results of this research would indicate that the method of contrast, which has worked successfully for linguistic scholars, has some flaws when applied to the task of developing reading vocabularies.

Isolation of Phonemes

It seems accurate to say that the isolation of phonemes from words is the aspect of phonics instruction that has received the sharpest as well as the greatest amount of criticism. You will recall from earlier pages in this chapter that the criticism reflects linguists' contentions that phonemes have no existence outside words; that every phoneme is a class or range of sounds rather than a single, unchanging one; and that attempts to isolate phonemes from words result in serious distortions.

In classrooms, the isolation that has been severely criticized can sometimes be heard when sounds are first being identified for children. ("You can hear the sound that *t* stands for if you listen to the beginning sound in words like *toy, take, tall, ten*. Can someone say that sound?") Isolation al:o is evident when individual sounds are synthesized into words (a→ac→act).

The illustrations just cited suggest the need to discuss the isolation of phonemes, or sounds, within two different contexts; that is, within the context of initial instruction about any given phoneme and, secondly, within the context of using phonemes to decode words. First, though, it seems best to deal with the reasons why linguists say phonemes cannot and should not be isolated and, afterward, to react from the point of view of one concerned with phonics instruction.

Isolation of Phonemes: From the Linguist's Point of View. Probably the first comment to make regarding linguists' observations about phonemes is that I am hardly in a position to dispute them. That is, not being a phonetician, I am not able to make an academic judgment about their contentions. Nonetheless, I *am* able to hear spoken language—which is the concern of the phonetician—and in the process to gather evidence for some of the points he makes. For example, I am aware that in the flow of spoken language, the phonemes composing words are articulated with such speed that it would not be possible to reproduce them apart from those words. Consequently, were you to say aloud a simple sentence like *The dog is sitting in the corner*, I would not be able to isolate any of the phonemes composing those seven spoken words and reproduce them in a way that would be an exact duplicate of what you said. Thus, I both understand and agree with the following linguistic observation:

> It is part of the very essence of language that sounds are uttered in very rapid sequences which become words. Each sound has such a fleeting existence that it is not truly reproducible outside the context of a word. Wresting it out of its natural place makes it something different, altering its length and the amount of breath put into it, and sometimes making it into a syllable by the addition of another sound (Stott, 1970, p. 11).

Having already agreed with this observation about spoken language and the phonemes composing it, let me also point out that if every child could learn everything he needed to know about decoding without ever having phonemes isolated for him, there would be no need to discuss isolation in this book. The fact is, however, that for some children and for some words, isolation seems both necessary and helpful. Before discussing those children and those words, let me first consider isolation within the context of phonics instruction.

Isolation of Phonemes: From the Point of View of Phonics. The first fact to be underscored within this context is that what is taught about phonemes is applied not to "flowing language" but to one word at a time; specifically, to a word that is unfamiliar in its written form.[6] Admittedly, even when only one word is being considered, its phonemes still are one thing when realized in that word and another when pronounced individually. Nonetheless, I hold to the point of view that for most phonemes the discrepancies need not be so great as to cause problems for the decoder. And, after all, decoding ability—not linguistic scholarship—is what phonics is all about.

That isolated phonemes need not always be seriously distorted is especially true of the vowels. In fact, pronouncing any of the single vowels or the diphthongs apart from words results in sounds that appear—at least to one who is not a phonetician—to be very much like what is heard when they appear in words. This is especially true when the words are not part of quickly moving speech but, instead, are being considered one at a time, as is the case when letter-sound relationships are used for decoding. Consonant sounds, on the other hand, are apt to be more distorted. This is particularly true of the stop sounds; that is, of /b/, /d/, /g/, /k/, /p/, and /t/. Even with them, careful pronunciations can reduce distortions at least somewhat.

To summarize, then, the assumption of this book is that isolation of phonemes is not something that must be avoided at all costs in phonics instruction. Stated positively, it takes the position that whenever circumstances suggest that such isolation might be helpful, it should be used. Possible circumstances will now be discussed in relation to, first, the identification of phonemes and, second, their use in decoding.

Isolation of Phonemes: For Identification. Over the years, phonemes have been identified in phonics instruction both inductively and deductively. (The two procedures will be discussed in Chapter 4.) Because inductive instruction resembles more closely the methodology recommended by the linguist-critic and because it clearly allows for a choice between isolation and no isolation, let me use that in this discussion.

Typically, when phonemes are identified inductively, attention goes to words in which they appear in the initial position. For example, if a teacher decides to teach the phoneme associated with *s*, she might choose to use words like:

> see
>
> sun
>
> sat

---

[6] To make this point is not to overlook a fact discussed in Chapter 1; namely, that a context—for instance, the sentence in which the unknown word appears—often helps with correct identification. Even when that is the case, however, the unknown word still is being considered apart from the flow of language.

Once words like these are read aloud, a comment would be made about the fact that all begin with the same letter but, too, with the same sound—the sound that s stands for in words. After asking the children to listen for that beginning sound, the teacher would read the words again. Then, in order to learn whether they were able to hear the sound, she might ask the children to try to think of other words that begin the same way; that is, with the same sound. If they respond with examples like "salt," "supper," "said," and "sorry," they are displaying evidence not only of having heard /s/ but also of having understood the meaning of "beginning sound." With such children isolation hardly is necessary. Instead, a next step would be to help them use their knowledge of this letter-sound association to decode unfamiliar words.

But what about the children who might not be able to hear /s/ in selected words even when many are used and many questions are asked about them? These children can hardly be overlooked, for, especially when phonics instruction is just beginning, they are not uncommon. With them, it is suggested, pronouncing /s/ apart from words will not only *not* cause problems—it will be helpful. In fact, it will be helpful not only in identifying this sound so that it can eventually be used in decoding but, in addition, it will help these same children understand the meaning of "beginning sound." That is, it will begin to clarify what is meant by requests like, "Can you think of words that begin with the sound that you hear at the beginning of *see, sun, sat?*"

One other point must be underscored right away. To take the position that some children require an explicit identification of a phoneme through isolation is *not* to support what sometimes takes place in classrooms. Here I refer to unfortunate practices like having children drill with "suh-suh-suh" (an unnecessary distortion, by the way) even after they have demonstrated an awareness of /s/. And I also have in mind teacher-comments that suggest the sound recorded by r is "er," by cl is "cul," and so on. It is just such practices that merit criticism, and not only from linguists.

Isolation of Phonemes: For Decoding. Once children are successful in learning about the sound that s (or any other letter) stands for in words, they are ready to use that association to decode unfamiliar words. More specifically, if they can read something like *come*, they are ready to decode *some* through what is called in phonics an "initial consonant substitution." Or, if words like *it* and *and* are known, using what is called an "initial consonant addition" will help identify *sit* and *sand.*

As these illustrations demonstrate, phonics instruction also employs the method of contrast (*come-some, it-sit, and-sand*), although it has not been customary to refer to it as such. In any case, and regardless of the name assigned to the procedure, it does not require that phonemes be isolated. What does require this, however, is a situation in which a written word needs to be identified, but it is unrelated to all the other words a child is able to read. Since *act* has been referred to before, let me continue to use that as an illustration of a time when isolation is required for successful decoding.

For this discussion the assumptions are that *act* is unfamiliar to a child in its written form; that he does not know words that bear some phonetic relationship to *act* (e.g., *fact*); and, thirdly, that he needs to know what it says. When all these are not just assumptions but facts, the point of view taken in this book is that synthesizing three phonemes can result in a correct identification. Specifically, if the sound called the short sound of *a* was learned with words like *and* and *add*; if the sound called the hard sound of *c* was learned with words like *car* and *cut*; and if the sound associated with *t* was learned with the help of words like *take* and *turn*, the contention is that children can and should be taught to start decoding *act* with an isolated phoneme to which others will be added (a→ac→act). The result should be a correct identification of *act*.

In summary, several points can be made about the isolation of phonemes. First, it is recognized that the way phonemes are realized in words cannot be exactly duplicated when those same phonemes are pronounced alone. This is especially true of consonants. Second, it also is recognized that some teachers isolate phonemes in their phonics instruction even when this is unnecessary. The hope is that this will become less common. Finally, it is asserted that there are circumstances when isolation is both necessary and helpful. Details about such circumstances will appear in subsequent chapters.

Chapter 3

THE CONTENT OF PHONICS INSTRUCTION

Phonics instruction has one goal: to teach children how to figure out the pronunciation of unfamiliar written words by using the relationship that exists between phonemes and graphemes. Since phonics does not offer help with meanings, it is productive only with words already known in their spoken form. Or, as Roger Brown (1958) has put it, "If the word that is unfamiliar in printed form is also unfamiliar in spoken form the reader who can sound it out will not understand the word any better than the reader who cannot sound it . . ." (p. 69).

With our language, the productivity of phonics is further limited by the irregularity to be found in the spellings of some words. More specifically, because there is not always a consistent match between spellings and pronunciations, phonics is not able to offer children rules that always work. Instead, it simply deals with observations that have been made about the way *most* words are spelled and pronounced. It thus teaches generalizations which, when applied to unknown words, lead to their correct identity most but not all of the time. Flexibility in that application, therefore, is essential. In fact, classroom observations point out repeatedly that one obvious difference between the good and the poor decoder is the flexibility with which the former uses generalizations.[1]

[1] How to foster this necessary flexibility will be treated in Chapter 4.

PHONICS GENERALIZATIONS

Most of the generalizations taught in phonics deal with letter-sound relationships (e.g., one vowel in a closed syllable generally records its short sound). What statements of these generalizations say pertains to syllables rather than to words; consequently some generalizations offer guidelines for dividing unknown words into syllables (e.g., when two consonants are preceded and followed by vowels, there usually is a syllabic division between the consonants). Whether a syllable is stressed or not can have an effect on the sounds its letters record. Therefore other generalizations deal with the syllables likely to be stressed in multisyllabic words (e.g., in two-syllable roots, the first syllable generally is stressed).

Whether considering sounds, syllabication, or stress, all the generalizations deal with *visual cues*. That is, they focus on single letters, letter combinations, and the sequence with which they appear in words. More importantly, they tell how these visual cues offer help with word identification.

Because attempts to identify words must often begin with a consideration of syllabication, that topic will be dealt with first.

SYLLABICATION

The importance of dividing an unknown word into syllables before its identification is attempted is not always apparent in beginning instruction because at that point the majority of the words that have to be learned have only one syllable. At that point, too, many new words can be decoded by using words that are already familiar along with phonic substitutions (run→sun) or additions (and→hand). As new words become longer and less obviously related to known words, however, the importance of starting the decoding process with syllabication becomes clear. This is why the discussion of generalizations will begin with those that have something to say about syllables.

What Is A Syllable?

To be noted first of all is that linguists have something to say about syllables. Hall (1961), for instance, has observed:

> Everyone agrees that there are such things as syllables in English speech, and that every vowel phoneme is the center (or "nucleus") of a syllable . . . . For our purposes, it is . . . important to notice that, in English speech, there is no clear boundary between one syllable and the next, as there is in, say, Italian or Spanish. Especially with a single consonant phoneme between two vowels, it is not possible to say to which syllable the consonant belongs: in a word like *demon*, the lowest point of sonority between the two syllables comes smack in the middle

of the consonant phoneme /m/, and we cannot say that the /m/ belongs more with the preceding syllable than it does with the one following (p. 12).

Later in the same book Hall says:

> . . . we especially need to recognize that the hyphenations and syllable-divisions set forth in our dictionaries are very largely arbitrary, and that they therefore do not, in fact cannot have, by the very nature of the situation, any absolute validity (p. 31).

Wardhaugh (1966), another linguist, makes a similar point when he writes:

> Although the number of syllables in an English utterance can be fairly easily determined, the precise point at which one syllable may be said to end and another begin is often impossible to determine . . . . The result is that the syllable divisions recorded in a written text are made according to convention and are essentially arbitrary (p. 786).

Apparent in all the material just quoted is that the linguist's primary concern is for oral language. And every user of oral language is as aware as is the linguist that there is no clear and certain demarcation between the syllables of his speech. Nonetheless, for dealing with written language—in particular for decoding individual words—consideration of syllables is helpful and sometimes even mandatory.

Linquists might not agree with this point of view. In fact one among them, Charles Fries, treats syllabication surprisingly lightly in *Linguistics and Reading* (1963). After discussing in considerable detail the use of both spelling patterns and the method of contrast to teach reading vocabularies, he observes:

> The word-patterns represented by this very large set of spelling patterns are all single syllable words. But these syllables occur very frequently as parts of multisyllable words (p. 177).

This observation immediately prompts one to compare single syllable and multi-syllable pairs of words like *hot* and *hotel* and *cab* and *cable* because such pairings clearly show the significance of syllabication for the sound a letter records. It is because of this significance that phonics instruction deals with syllables.

Admittedly, generalizations about syllabication hardly take into account such technical details as "sonority." But—and this point has been made before—it must also be remembered that phonics is pragmatic. It tries to teach what will work. That is, it tries to teach whatever will offer children help in decoding words. With that goal in mind, the contention of this book is that generalizations about syllabication ought to get attention. Before dealing with them, there is the need to define "syllable" as that term is used in this book.

One description that is used says the syllable is the unit of pronunciation. Such a description explains why syllabication has relevance for decoding. Another description emphasizes another feature that makes it relevant: A syllable contains a vowel sound, which might or might not be combined with consonant sounds. Thus, each of the following is one syllable and, in fact, could be no more than one:

u　　us　　rus　　rust　　thrust

It happens that each of these five syllables contains a single vowel letter; that is not always so, however, as can be seen in each of the following one-syllable words:

meal　　tape　　caught　　loud　　boil　　voice　　seize

In *meal, tape,* and *caught,* there are two vowel letters but just one vowel sound. In *loud* and *boil,* there also are two vowel letters which, in each case, record diphthongs. Although linguists say a diphthong is a combination of vowel and semivowel sounds, diphthongs are treated in phonics as single sounds. For that reason words like *loud* and *boil* are considered to have, as do other syllables, one vowel sound. The same would be true for a word like *voice* in which the first two vowel letters stand for a diphthong, whereas the third does not record any sound. In the case of *seize,* the *e* records its long sound, and both the *i* and the final *e* are "silent."

The various examples of syllables can serve to describe another of their features. This description catalogues syllables as "open" and "closed." An *open syllable* ends with a vowel sound, a *closed syllable* with a consonant sound. To be noted, by the way, is that the distinction is based on final sounds, not letters. This is why the syllables *u* and *high* are considered to be open, whereas all the other examples listed earlier— including *tape* and *voice*—would be classified as closed.

Phonics instruction considers syllables in still another way as it employs terms like *initial sound, medial sound,* and *final sound.* With a syllable such as *rus,* the *r* would be said to record its initial or beginning sound; the *u* its medial or middle sound; and the *s* its final or last sound. Since a syllable can contain just a single sound—always a vowel—not all syllables have all three sounds. Nonetheless, all three are possible and are referred to in certain aspects of phonics instruction.

To sum up, then, the syllable is of basic importance to phonics because it is the unit of pronunciation. In fact, it is on the syllable, not the word, that phonics generalizations focus. A vowel sound is its nucleus in the sense that every syllable contains a vowel sound, to which consonant sounds are often added. When other sounds *are* added, the various parts of the syllable are sometimes referred to as initial, medial, and final. When the final sound is a consonant, the syllable would be classified as closed. When the final sound is a vowel, it would be considered an open syllable.

How syllables can be identified with the help of visual cues will now be dealt with via statements of generalizations. As all the generalizations are discussed, keep in mind that they are considering written language, not oral, and that they are to be used with words that are not recognized in their written form.

Syllable Generalizations

One visual cue for syllabication, the presence of one vowel letter in a word, is indirectly highlighted in a generalization mentioned earlier:

> Every syllable has a vowel sound.

With guidance from this generalization, a child would know immediately that unfamiliar words such as *so* or *rust* or *stretch* could be no more than one syllable because each contains only one vowel letter. Once the child is aware that *qu* is treated as if it were a consonant letter, he would also know that unfamiliar words like *quit* or *quest* could also be no more than one syllable. Or, for example, after an unknown word like *hectic* has been divided into the two syllables *hec* and *tic* (with the help of a generalization soon to be discussed), the child would also know that no further syllabication is possible with the help of the generalization: Every syllable has a vowel sound.

Another generalization also offers indirect help with syllabication. This one, again centering on a vowel letter as the important cue, states:

> When other vowels appear in a word, a final *e*
> usually is silent.[2]

Using this generalization as his guideline, a child could decide with some certainty that unknown words like *tape* and *role* have only one vowel sound and thus would be one-syllable words. (With words like *me* and

---

[2] Reflecting the linguistic influence, this generalization sometimes appears in a form that avoids the reference to silent letters. (Since letters do not have sounds, says the linguist-critic, how can they be "silent"?) Facts are not available to answer the question, Which form will have the greater positive effect on a child's decoding ability? And that, after all, is *the* important question.

she, the final *e* could not be silent because it is the only letter available to record the necessary vowel sound.)

The likely presence of other "silent vowels" also helps the decoder with decisions about syllabication. For instance, by applying a generalization concerned with letter-sound relationships (when there are two vowels together, the first often records its long sound while the second is silent), a child could make at least a tentative decision that such unfamiliar words as *meet* and *coal* also are only one syllable.

The two generalizations cited thus far show how considerations of syllables and sounds often go on simultaneously. Other generalizations deal separately with syllabication. This is so of the following one, in which both vowel and consonant letters are the cues offering assistance to the decoder:

> When two consonants are between two vowels, a syllabic division often occurs between the consonants. For example:
>
> num ber   pic nic   tor ment   lim pid

Although this particular generalization focuses only on syllabication, it can also have meaning for the sounds letters record. For instance, its immediate use with unknown words like *number* (*num ber*) or *combine* (*com bine*) would avoid problems for children who have been taught or simply have noticed that *mb* only records the sound associated with *m* (*lamb, dumb, climb*). In this case the problem would be avoided because the generalization points out that the *m* and *b* are in different syllables in both *number* and *combine*. The same illustrations also show how "looking for little words in big words" (*numb* in *number*; *comb* in *combine*) creates more pronunciation problems than it solves and for that reason should be avoided.

The generalization stated above, as it singles out two consonants that are both preceded and followed by vowels, will sometimes be applied to words in which the two adjacent consonants are the same letter; for example, to words like *dinner, hello,* and *support*. With such words the double consonant often signals help not only with syllabication but also with the sound the previous vowel is likely to record. This is illustrated in such pairs of words as:

dinner	diner
pinning	pining
tapped	taped

One other comment needs to be made about words in which the two successive consonants are the same letter. Generally, only one records a sound; more specifically, the one in the stressed syllable:

dín ɣer   lát ɣer   heɣló   suɣ póse

When the identical adjacent consonants happen to be *c* or *g*, another pattern is possible, depending upon the letter that follows. In words like *accord* or *wiggle*, the pronunciation pattern is the one mentioned above (*aɣ córd; wig ɣle*). In words like *accent* and *suggest*, the *c*'s and *g*'s continue to be in separate syllables (*ac cent; sug gest*) but each letter in the pair records a different sound.[3]

The next generalization about syllabication again singles out both vowels and consonants as the relevant cue:

> When a consonant is between two vowels, a syllabic division often occurs between the preceding vowel and the consonant.[4] For example:
>
> o ver   hu man   to tem   spi ral

The significance of considering syllabication *prior to* sounds can be reillustrated with the above generalization. For instance, the child who begins to decode words like *away* or *aware* by first considering their likely syllables would not assign to *aw* the single sound this combination of letters commonly records in such words as *raw* or *awful* because the syllabic divisions suggested by the generalization show *a* and *w* to be in different syllables (*a way; a ware*). Nor would the child be likely to conclude that the sound of *dig* will be in *digest* (*di gest*) or that the sound of *beg* will occur in words like *begin* or *beget* (*be gin; be get*).

In discussing the various generalizations pertaining to syllables, it should be remembered that more than one sometimes is needed to complete syllabication. If an unknown word were *mercury*, for example, one of the generalizations already cited would suggest *mer cury*, and another would conclude with *mer cu ry*.

One more generalization about syllabication is important because of the number of words to which it can be applied. This focuses on a consonant plus *le* as the helpful cue:

---

[3] The two sounds that *c* and *g* each record are discussed in a later section of the chapter.

[4] A notable exception to this generalization is found in words in which the consonant is *x*. With these, the *x* and the preceding vowel are in the same syllable. For example: *exit* (*ex it*), *axis* (*ax is*), *oxen* (*ox en*).

When a word ends in *le* preceded by a consonant, that consonant plus the *le* constitutes
a syllable. For example:

a ble   pur ple   spin dle   nee dle

With these kinds of words, the vowel sound in the syllable spelled with a
consonant plus *le* is the *schwa* sound. This is like the short *u* sound,
which is heard at the beginning of *us* and *up*. Thus, the sound of *ble* is
"bəl," the sound of *ple* is "pəl," and so on.

The structure of words also has relevance for syllabication. One
example is highlighted in the next generalization:

Prefixes and suffixes usually are separate syllables. For example:

un cap   fore warn   care ful   count less

The first two words in these examples have prefixes that are still active
in our language. Other words (e.g., *alone, below, deceive*) have prefixes
that are inactive and have been absorbed into the root. For that reason
they are referred to as "absorbed prefixes" (Deighton, 1959). Absorbed
or not, they still follow the syllabication pattern highlighted in the
generalization, which suggests that most prefixes are separate syllables
(*a lone, be low, de ceive*).

One more generalization pertains both to the structure of a word and
to syllabication. It singles out an inflectional ending:

When the inflectional ending *ed* is added to
roots ending in *d* or *t*, it forms a separate syllable. Otherwise it adds a sound to the root
but not a syllable. For example:

land ed   point ed   stayed   jumped

STRESS

The correct identification of a word is achieved only when the right
syllable is stressed. (How incorrect stress alters pronunciation often
becomes apparent in the speech of individuals for whom English is a
second language.) Not many generalizations are available to help but,
fortunately, the scarcity presents no major problems because figuring out
the sounds of syllables commonly leads to a correct decision about
which syllable is to receive special stress. More specifically, decoding the
likely sounds of the syllables in such words as *able* and *purple* results

in an automatic awareness of which of the two syllables gets the stress. (Such a sequence of events is possible, of course, only when the words being decoded are familiar in their spoken form.)

It happens that there is a generalization that offers at least indirect help with stress in words like *able* and *purple:*

> Final syllables spelled with a consonant plus *le* are not stressed. For example:
>
>   crádle   rúffle   cápable   exámple

Another generalization about stress singles out root words:

> In two-syllable roots, stress is usually given to the first syllable. For example:
>
>   wíndow   pícture   márry   páper

Another generalization deals with roots through attention to derived and inflected words. [A derived word, or derivative, comprises a root and a prefix (*untie*) or a root and a suffix (*spotless*) or a root and both a prefix and a suffix (*retellable*). An inflected word comprises a root and an inflectional ending (*doing, softly*).] This particular generalization says of stress:

> In derived or inflected words, the stress falls on the root. For example:
>
>   shóeless   púlling   alóne   miscóunt   retéllable

That stress can affect the sounds that letters record is still another important point for decoders to keep in mind. Especially common in English is the shift of vowel sounds to the *schwa* sound, when they appear in unstressed syllables. (See page 36 for the earlier discussion of this sound.) Underlined letters in the words below illustrate what is a very common pattern:

>   píl<u>o</u>t   séd<u>ime</u>nt   <u>a</u>fféct   pl<u>a</u>tóon

Still one other point about stress needs to be made. This is the fact that certain words serve in more than one grammatical role; consequently, they can have more than one stress pattern. Recently, this feature of our language was heralded in the motto printed on a passing garbage truck: "We refuse no refuse." Generally, when words serve as both nouns and verbs (e.g., *refuse, survey, conduct, insult, digest*), the first syllable is stressed when it is a noun, the second when it functions as a verb.

LETTER-SOUND RELATIONSHIPS

That we have letter-sound relationships, or, as they are referred to in some newer materials, grapheme-phoneme correspondences, reflects our use of an alphabetic writing system. Helping readers use those relationships to decode unknown words constitutes a major concern of phonics instruction.

What sometimes complicates that instruction is the lack of consistency in the sounds letters record. This is especially characteristic of what have come to be called "the vowels" (*a, e, i, o, u*). In fact, it is the lack of consistency that sometimes prompts teachers and/or instructional materials to deal initially with what have come to be called "the consonants" (the other 21 letters).[5]

On this and the following pages, attention will first be given to the consonant sounds and the way they are recorded with both single letters and digraphs. Then the various vowel sounds found in our language will be identified and discussed.

Consonants

What single consonants record is fairly consistent, at least when a comparison is made with the vowels. The words listed below begin with seventeen of the consonants and demonstrate the sound each commonly represents:

big	lap	tall
day	me	very
fat	not	with
he	pan	yes
jet	run	zoo
key	see	

Emphasis on consistency is not meant to minimize the variation found among consonants. For instance, the intent is not to cloud the fact that *s*

---

[5] As Chapter 2 pointed out, "vowel" and "consonant" are phonetic classifications referring to speech sounds, not letters. However, because the letters *a, e, i, o,* and *u* commonly record vowel sounds, they have come to be called "the vowels." The same commentary applies to the 21 letters called "the consonants." In this book, "vowel" and "consonant" will refer to letters if only because "vowel letter" and "consonant letter" become unnecessarily awkward at times. On the other hand, the two classifications of sounds will be referred to as "vowel sound" and "consonant sound" to indicate that in this case the reference is to a sound (phoneme), not a letter (grapheme).

records both /s/ and /z/, as in *tops* and *plays*; and, for example, that *d* can stand for /d/ and /t/, as in *peeled* and *passed*. Nor are "silent" consonants being overlooked as they appear in such words as *debt, lamb, gnaw, oh,* and *knot.*[6] Rather, the intent is simply to point out that most single consonants are fairly consistent in what they record and, further, that some of the apparent inconsistencies follow certain patterns. For example, it is common for *h* to record the sound heard at the beginning of *he,* but *h* can also be silent when it appears in initial position (*hour, heir*); when it follows a vowel sound (*oh, ah*); and when it follows *r* (*rhyme, rhubarb*) or *g* (*high, caught*).

To some extent, similar comments could be made about other single consonants. For instance, *k* usually records the sound heard at the beginning of *key,* but we also are accustomed to its "silence" when it is followed by *n* (*knight, knot*). The point is that the seventeen consonants appearing at the beginning of the listed words often enough record the initial sounds heard in those words to warrant instruction with those letter-sound associations. In fact, attention to them usually constitutes initial instruction in phonics.

The listed words, you probably noticed, included *yes,* in which *y* functions as a consonant. The way *y* and also *w* function as vowels will be discussed later. The four consonants not listed (*c, g, q, x*) will get attention now.

C, G

Both *c* and *g* commonly record two different sounds, referred to in phonics as "hard" and "soft" sounds.[7] These are impressionistic descriptions in the sense that the hard sounds for both letters appear to be harsher than the soft sounds. Because classroom observations reveal that children can assign their own definitions to "hard" (difficult), some explanation of the descriptions should be given when the sounds are taught.

For *c,* the hard sound is the one heard at the beginning of *cat* and *curl,* which is to say it is the sound customarily associated with *k.* In fact, in final position this sound often is recorded with both *c* and *k* (*pick*) but not always (*hectic*). Infrequently, *ch* is used (*chord, ache, echo*).

The soft sound of *c* is heard at the beginning of *cent* and *city.* Again you will notice that this sound, too, is associated with another letter, in

---

[6] Some instructional materials now say it is the combination *kn* that records the initial sound in a word like *knot.* Once more, this reflects the move away from references to "silent" letters.

[7] When each is likely to occur will be explained later. For now the goal is simply to identify the sounds.

this case *s*. Thus, *c* commonly stands for two sounds, both of which are typical sounds for two other letters:

C

Hard Sound	Examples
/k/	call, come, cot

Soft Sound	Examples
/s/	cell, cigar, city

What is called the "soft" sound of *g* also is associated with another letter, in this instance *j*. It is heard at the beginning of such words as *gym* and *gentle*. The hard sound can be heard in words like *go* and *gate*. In some others, such as *guide* and *guard*, the *gu* combine to record the hard sound; this only happens, however, when there is another vowel in addition to the *u*. Consequently, this would hold for words like *guess* and *guilt* but not for words like *gum* and *gull*, in which the *u* records the vowel sound that every syllable must have.

The two sounds commonly represented by *g* are illustrated below:

G

Hard Sound	Examples
/g/	gag, go, gulf

Soft Sound	Examples
/j/	gem, gist, gym

Q

The letter *q* is always followed by *u*. Together, *qu* records the blend and single sound shown below:

Qu

Sounds	Examples
/kw/	queen
/k/	bouquet

In phonics instruction, *qu* is treated as a unit, more specifically as a single consonant. Thus, words like *quit* and *quake* ought to be seen by children as paralleling words like *hit* and *wake*.

X

Like *c* and *q*, *x* makes no special contribution to our writing system in the sense that it stands for sounds commonly recorded by other letters. This is illustrated in the examples below, which show how *x* can stand for a single sound as well as for two different blends:

X

Sounds	Examples
/gz/	exact
/ks/	taxi
/z/	anxiety

Compared to other consonants, *x* appears infrequently in words. This is why attention to the sounds it can record is usually delayed.

Consonant Digraphs

Using the literal definition of digraph (two letters), there are two types of consonant digraphs that need to be discussed. The first group gets attention in phonics for the sake of efficiency. That is, certain pairs of consonants appear in words sufficiently frequently that the ability to deal with them together speeds up the decoding process. These particular digraphs, now referred to as "clusters" in some of the newer instructional materials, are listed below:

Consonant Clusters   *blends*

bl	fl	sc	st
br	fr	sk	sw
cl	gl	sl	tr
cr	gr	sm	tw
dr	pl	sn	
dw	pr	sp	

Each letter in these clusters records its own sound. For instance, when *bl* appears in a word like *blue*, the *b* stands for one sound and the *l* for another. Together, they record a sequence or blend of two sounds: /bl/. It is this characteristic that distinguishes this type of consonant digraph from another.

The other type of digraph is more unique and special in that the digraphs constituting this group record sounds that are different from those associated with either letter constituting the pair. Let me show these six digraphs as well as the way they record single sounds, each of which must be dealt with as a unit by decoders:

Consonant Digraphs

th (the; thin)
ph (phone)

gh (rough)
sh (show)
ch (chair; chef)
ng (sing)

As the above illustrations point out, these digraphs do not record blended sounds.[8] For that reason they are dealt with as a unit, not for something like efficiency, but rather out of necessity. A few further comments about each follow.

As the list shows, the digraph *th* stands for two different sounds. One, the voiced sound, is heard in words like *the*, *thus*, and *father*. The other, the voiceless sound, is found in such words as *thin*, *thirst*, and *with*. For any who might have difficulty hearing the difference between the two, the following contrasts should be helpful:

Voiced Sound	*Voiceless Sound*
thy	thigh
bathe	bath
breathe	breath
either	ether

The next two digraphs appearing in the list, *ph* and *gh*, record the same sound, one associated with the single consonant *f*. The combination *ph* represents it in both initial and final positions (*phone, graph*). The combination *gh* stands for it in final position (*rough, laugh*). In fact, when *gh* is in initial position (*ghost, ghetto*), the *g* records its hard sound and the *h* is silent. Sometimes, too, *gh* itself is silent: *eight, high, caught*.

The sound that *sh* stands for in words like *show* and *wash* is a common one in our language and is spelled in a great many ways. For example: *sugar, action, ocean, efficient, mission, mansion, issue*.

Except in words of obvious French origin (e.g., *chef, chauffeur, champagne, chaise, chamois*), the digraph *ch* usually represents the sound heard at the beginning of *chair* and at the beginning and end of *church*. When this is a final sound, however, it is more commonly spelled *tch* (*catch, pitch*).

The next digraph in the list, *ng*, records what linguists call a "nasal" sound. In our language this pair of letters never appears in initial position

---

[8] As was noted in Chapter 2, phoneticians classify the sound recorded by *ch* in *chair* as a close blend of two sounds. Since this blend is not easily heard by children—or by adults for that matter—what *ch* stands for in *chair* is considered in phonics to be a single sound.

but, instead, follows vowels (*song, length*). Thus, the sound it records is part of such combinations as *ing, ang, ung*. The same nasal sound, by the way, can also be represented by *n* alone when *n* precedes /g/, /k/, or /z/. This occurs fairly frequently and is illustrated in words like *bank* and *ink* and also in *hunger, anchor, banquet*, and *anxiety*.

One comment needs to be made about a consonant digraph that does not appear in the list. I refer to *wh*. Although some include it as one of the "special" digraphs, it is not listed here because what it records is different from the requirements already mentioned: two consonants recording a single sound that is not like the sound associated with either of the letters constituting the pair. To be more specific, in *who* the *wh* stands for /h/. What it records in a word like *which* depends upon the dialect of the person saying it. In some dialect areas *which* and *witch* are pronounced the same, meaning that the *wh* in *which* simply stands for /w/. But in other areas it records /hw/. Keeping in mind the three possibilities (/h/, /w/, /hw/), this particular digraph clearly does not belong with the other six.

One further comment needs to be made about the other six. This pertains to syllabication; specifically to the fact that the six digraphs function as if they were single consonants when unfamiliar words are being divided into syllables. For syllabication purposes, for instance, words like *anchor* (*an chor*) and *panther* (*pan ther*) parallel words like *number* (*num ber*) and *picnic* (*pic nic*). Similarly, words like *ether* (*e ther*) and *ashamed* (*a shamed*) follow the syllabication pattern of words like *silent* (*si lent*) and *female* (*fe male*).

Vowels

Just how important vowel sounds are becomes obvious when it is remembered that every syllable contains one. This is why phonics instruction gives attention to vowel sounds as soon as possible even though —and this was pointed out earlier—how they are represented in our written language varies considerably.

Generalizations are available to help children cope with the variability; they will be discussed in a later section of this chapter. The goal now is simply to identify the vowel sounds.

Long Vowel Sounds.[9] Let me begin with the five long vowel sounds because to know the names of the five vowel letters is also to know these sounds. They appear in initial position in the following:

age   eat   ice   old   use

Short Vowel Sounds. The five short vowel sounds are more difficult

[9] To review the earlier discussion of "long" and "short," see pages 10–11.

for children to perceive and remember; in addition, they are characterized by dialect differences. They can be heard at the beginning of each of these words:

as   end   it   odd   up

It will be recalled that the short *u* sound is like what is called the *schwa* sound. Occurring very frequently in unstressed syllables, the *schwa* can be heard in words like the following, in which the underlined letters record it:

agaín   sága   ómen   sécret
návigate   córridor   pílot   collápse

Sometimes, but not as often, vowel sounds in unstressed syllables are reduced to the short *i* sound. This is so, for example, in the following words:

mánage   defíne   revólt   trúmpet

As the underlined letters suggest, it is *e* that most often represents this deemphasized sound.

Y *Functioning as a Vowel.* In any discussion of long and short vowel sounds the letter *y* must be accounted for, even though it is a consonant. It is relevant to such a discussion because it functions as a consonant only when appearing at the beginning of a syllable (*yes, canyon*); otherwise it functions as a vowel and records the long and short sounds described in the following generalizations.

> When *y* is in a closed syllable that has no vowel letter, it usually records the short *i* sound. For example:
>
> gym   myth   lymph   Cynthia
>
> When *y* records the final sound in a one-syllable word, it usually stands for the long *i* sound. For example:
>
> my   dye   try   fly
>
> When *y* records the final sound in a multi-

syllabic word, it usually stands for the long
e sound.[10] For example:

softly   crusty   fairy   charity

To sum up, *y* can record the long and short *i* sounds as well as the long
e sound. What it is likely to represent depends upon its placement in
the syllable or word, and also on whether there are vowel letters present.
   Diphthongs. Diphthongs, as the previous chapter explained, are considered by phoneticians to be close blends of vowel and semivowel
sounds. For instance, the underlined letters in the words below would be
said to stand for blends:

o̲il   bo̲y̲   o̲u̲t   ho̲w̲

That each of these diphthongs *is* a blend is not readily apparent to
children. This is why the sounds heard at the beginning of *oil* and *out*
are treated in phonics as single sounds, although they are still referred
to as diphthongs.[11]
   As the illustrative words demonstrated, diphthongs are represented by
vowels plus *y* and *w* functioning as vowels. Thus *oi*, *oy*, *ou*, and *ow* can
be thought of as special vowel digraphs in the sense that they often record a diphthong. Whenever these diphthongs appear in words (*voice,
oyster, ouch, tower*), the vowel digraphs representing them should be
treated by the decoder as if they were but one vowel letter. As was mentioned before, the sounds they stand for also are considered to be a single
sound rather than the close blend of two.
   Vowel Digraphs. Certain vowel digraphs that represent diphthongs
were discussed in the preceding section. Other vowel digraphs, however,
also need to be mentioned because they can stand for three vowel sounds
that have not yet been identified. They can be heard in the following
words and are represented by the underlined digraphs:

a̲u̲to   la̲w̲   o̲o̲ze   bo̲o̲k

The single sound recorded by *au* in *auto* and by *aw* in *law* is the same.
What double-*o* stands for in *ooze* is referred to as its long sound; what it
records in *book* is referred to as its short sound. Because the long sound
occurs more frequently, that is the one a decoder would try out initially.

---

[10] When *y* appears in a multisyllabic word and records the final sound in a syllable
that is not the last one (e.g., *tycoon, cyclone*), it usually stands for the long *i* sound.
[11] Technically, the long sounds of *i* (*ice*) and *u* (*use*) also are diphthongs. This is
why *ew* in a word like *few* is said to represent a diphthong.

As a summary of what has been said thus far about sounds recorded by digraphs—both vowel and consonant digraphs—the following lists should be helpful:

Vowel Digraphs Representing Diphthongs	Some Other Vowel Digraphs	Consonant Digraphs
oi (oil)	au (auto)	th (the; thin)
oy (boy)	aw (law)	ph (phone)
ou (out)	oo (ooze; book)	gh (cough)
ow (owl)		ch (chap; chef)
		sh (she)
		ng (sing)

Factors Affecting Sounds Recorded by Letters

If there were perfect consistency in the relationship existing between letters and sounds, there would be no need to discuss how the same letter can stand for different sounds. Thus, there would be no need for this section of the chapter. As it is, a very important and necessary goal of phonics instruction is to help children learn how to deal with variability; that is, with the fact that certain letters of our alphabet commonly record more than one sound or, seemingly, no sound at all.

Fortunately for decoders, our writing system is not totally capricious—although to beginners in reading it might sometimes appear to be just that. Instead, there are certain spelling-pronunciation patterns, which will now be discussed through statements of generalizations. Like the earlier generalizations about syllabication and stress, these deal with visual cues, which, in this case, offer the decoder help in assigning sounds to certain letters. Like the other generalizations, too, they are not rules that always work. Rather, they are observations that highlight certain common but not inevitable spelling-pronunciation patterns.

Consonant Sounds. One common pattern helps the decoder assign sounds to *c* and *g*. It is described in the following generalizations:

> When *c* is followed within a syllable by *e*, *i*, or *y*, it usually records its soft sound. Otherwise the hard sound is common. For example:
>
> cent   cite   cyst
> curl   clam   cactus

> When *g* is followed within a syllable by *e* or

y, it usually records its soft sound.[12] Otherwise the hard sound is common. For example:

| gem | germ | gym | gypsy |
| gap | got | dig | wagon |

In the earlier discussion of consonant sounds, *q* and *x* were also singled out as representing a variety of sounds:

Q(u)	X
quaint /kw/	exact /gz/
bouquet /k/	taxi /ks/
	anxiety /z/

Frequency of occurrence can help the decoder deal with the variability shown above. In the case of *qu*, /kw/ is the common sound, especially when *qu* begins a word. With *x*, /z/ occurs almost never, whereas /ks/ is the most common sound, especially when *x* is the final letter in a syllable.

Vowel Sounds: One Vowel Letter. As would be expected, most of the generalizations pertaining to variability in letter-sound relationships focus on vowels rather than on consonants since they are the letters, either alone or in combination with other letters, that show the greatest variation in what they record. Five of the vowel sounds are referred to as the short sounds. When they are likely to occur is described in the following generalization:

> When there is one vowel in a syllable and it is not the final letter, it usually records its short sound. For example:
>
> add   stretch   cactus   napkin

This generalization points out that relevant, visual cues for decoding are not only letters but also the placement of those letters in a syllable. What this suggests, in turn, is the need for decoders to scan the *whole* of a syllable before assigning sounds to letters that tend to vary in what they record. In some of the newer instructional materials—this exemplifies

---

[12] When *i* follows *g* in a syllable, the soft sound and hard sound occur with about the same frequency. Each sound, therefore, would have to be tried out by the decoder to see which produces a word that makes sense in the context in which it is found. This is an example of the flexibility that was cited earlier as being an essential ingredient of successful decoding.

the linguistic influence—the importance of the whole syllable is brought out in the attention now given to spelling patterns. For instance, the last generalization cited is likely to be stated as: Most syllables with a c-v-c (consonant-vowel-consonant) pattern have short vowel sounds.

The importance of considering the whole of a syllable is reemphasized in the next generalization, which also deals with syllables that contain only one vowel letter:

> When *r* follows a single vowel in a syllable, the vowel plus *r* can record the three different sounds heard in *or*, *art*, and *her*. For example:

> word   warm   hurt   car

Additional reasons to consider the whole of a syllable that contains a single vowel—in this case *a*—are cited below:

> When double-*l* or *lk* follows *a* in a syllable, the *a* often records the vowel sound that is customarily represented by *aw* or *au*. For example:

> all   enthrall   walk   chalk

> When *a* is preceded by *w*, it records the sound heard in the following words:

> want   wad   watch   wasp

The need to pay special attention to what follows *i* in a syllable is highlighted by a generalization that says:

> When *i* is the only vowel and is followed in the syllable by *ld*, *nd*, *gn*, *gh*, or *ght*, it usually records its long sound. For example:

> mild   kind   sign   high   right

Finally, the need to notice what follows *o* is emphasized in this generalization:

> When *o* is the only vowel and is followed in

the syllable by *ld*, it usually records its long
sound. For example:

old   scold   behold

Because the sound a single vowel does stand for can be affected by
the letter or letters that follow, the newer phonics materials are now
giving much attention to what are called *phonograms*. Phonograms—
also referred to as graphemic bases—are clusters of letters, the first of
which is a vowel, that occur fairly frequently in syllables. They would
include such clusters as *-ip, -all, -ight*, and *-ang*. Individuals who promote
attention to phonograms see it as a way of making the decoding process
more efficient and, too, as a way of helping a child deal with the variability that characterizes what vowels record (Wylie and Durrell, 1970).

To summarize, it is important for the decoder to notice not only the
presence of one vowel in a syllable but, in addition, the letters that
precede and follow. What is the effect when no letter follows—that is,
when the single vowel is the final letter in the syllable—is described as
follows:

When there is one vowel in a syllable and it
is the final letter, it usually records its long
sound. For example:

go   hi   she   halo   silo

The special significance of the placement of a single vowel is underscored in such pairs of words as:

be   bed
go   got
hi   him
me   men

Contrasts like these are very helpful in teaching two of the more
important generalizations—both already cited—about single vowels and
the sounds they are likely to represent.

Vowel Sounds: Two Vowel Letters. Words (or syllables) containing
two vowel letters, one of which is a final *e*, were discussed earlier, when
syllabication was the concern. At that time the pertinent generalization was: When another vowel is in a word, a final *e* generally is silent.
The presence of the *e*, you will recall, was the cue suggesting that words
like *tape* and *role* would be single syllable words.

A final, silent *e* also offers help with the sound likely to be recorded by the other vowel in the syllable. In fact, final *e* is referred to as a *marker* because it so often signals this kind of assistance. How it can function as a marker for sounds is described as follows:

> When there are two vowels in a syllable, one of which is a final *e*, the first usually records its long sound and the final *e* is silent. For example:

cube   ode   strange   dye

In some newer materials—again this reflects the linguistic influence—"silent" letters tend to be dropping out of the picture. Thus, the above generalization might be verbalized as: Most syllables with a v-c-e (vowel-consonant-*e*) pattern have long vowel sounds.

When two vowels do appear in a syllable, the second one will not always be a final *e*. Nonetheless, a similar pronunciation pattern is common:

> When there are two adjacent vowels in a syllable, the first often records its long sound while the second is silent. For example:

coat   keep   plea   day

In the newer materials the trend is to say—using the above examples as illustrations—that *oa* records the long *o* sound, that *ee* records the long *e* sound, and so on. This reflects the new interest in spelling patterns as well as the move away from references to silent letters, both illustrating the linguistic influence.

Regardless of how generalizations are stated, more than the ability to count vowels is required for successful decoding. For example, two adjacent vowels might be what were referred to earlier as special digraphs —special in the sense that they often record diphthongs (*out, oil*) or single sounds that are different from the ten long and short vowel sounds (*auto, ooze, book*). One further complication is the possibility that the two adjacent vowels are in different syllables, in which case each would record a sound. This does not occur frequently, but is illustrated in words like:

duel   lion   giant   diet   Indian

As the examples demonstrate, a syllabic division is most likely to occur when the first of the two vowels is *i*.

What all these comments point out—again—is that phonic generalizations can only serve as guidelines, that is, as starting points in the decoding process. More specifically, if a syllable does contain two adjacent vowels that are not among those described as "special," the decoder can begin by applying the generalization: When there are two adjacent vowels they often stand for the long sound of the first one. If this does not work—that is, if it does not produce a word that makes sense—then a trial-and-error process needs to get under way. How to carry that on systematically will be discussed in Chapter 4.

There are still other generalizations or guidelines that can offer pronunciation help with syllables containing two vowel letters. One focuses on vowels that are followed by *re*:

> When a vowel is followed in a syllable by *re*,
> the vowel plus *re* usually record the sounds
> heard in the words: *dare, mere, hire, bore,*
> *cure.*

Earlier, a generalization suggested that a final *e* often signals a long sound for the previous vowel (e.g., *pile, cube*). Like the generalization just cited, however, the next one also highlights the need to notice more than just that final *e*:

> When a vowel is followed in a syllable by
> *nce, nge,* or *dge,* it often records its short
> sound. For example:

> dunce   prince   plunge   badge   judge

The above could be stated less specifically as: When a vowel is followed by two consonants plus final *e*, the short vowel sound usually occurs. As was brought out earlier, if the first of those two consonants is *r* (*large, purse*), the vowel and the *r* record special sounds.

Vowel Sounds: Three Vowel Letters. Not many syllables contain as many as three vowel letters. When this happens, the third is apt to be a final *e*. For example:

> voice   lounge   seize   freeze   raise

In the case of *voice* and *lounge*, the *oi* and *ou* record diphthongs. In the other three words, where there also are two adjacent vowels in addition to the final *e*, they record the long sound of the first vowel. Expectedly, in all the examples the final *e* does not stand for any additional sound.

A SUMMARY

What can be taught in phonics has been the focus of this chapter. As its pages have shown, this content deals with syllabication, letter-sound relationships, and stress. To help with all three, some generalizations are available. In each instance they single out cues that provide visual assistance for the decoding process.

The generalizations dealing with syllabication focus on certain sequences of letters within a word that offer help with decisions about syllable divisions. These decisions are of initial importance because the next set of generalizations used in decoding, those dealing with letter-sound relationships, deals with syllables, not words.

Just as the whole of a word must be scrutinized when syllabication is considered, so, too, must the whole of a syllable be scanned when sounds are being assigned to its letters. To help decoders systematize the scanning, other generalizations are available. Again, these give attention to visual cues—that is, to certain sequences of letters. They deal, for the most part, with vowels rather than consonants because the former vary more in what they record. In addition, these generalizations focus both on single letters and on digraphs.

Once syllabication and sounds are considered by the decoder, the next step, when the word being analyzed has more than one syllable, is to decide which of the syllables is to get special stress. Because of the inconsistent stress pattern of our language, it is fortunate that knowing syllables and sounds often automatically suggests a correct decision for stress. As with any feature of decoding, success with this last step is directly dependent on whether the word being analyzed is familiar to the decoder in its spoken form. This is why helping children to expand listening/speaking vocabularies is one of the best ways to ensure that they will be maximally successful decoders. Another way for teachers to foster success is to be thoroughly knowledgeable themselves about the content of phonics. The importance of this is the reason for the present chapter. How teachers can communicate that knowledge to others will be discussed in the next chapter.

Chapter 4

INSTRUCTIONAL PROCEDURES

With all the attention that is going to phonics, it might be necessary to start the present chapter with an admission of what ought to be obvious; namely, that reading comprises more than the ability to decode words. Or, to make the same point from a teacher's perspective, reading instruction is made up of much more than instruction in phonics.

Having recognized the incompleteness of phonics, let me also state explicitly the assumption of this book: Independence in figuring out the identity of words is one important requirement for success in reading. That is why this chapter gives detailed attention to instructional procedures for phonics.

CONTRIBUTORS TO SUCCESS

When to begin instructional procedures seems like the first question to raise. It also seems that the best answer can come through a consideration of what it takes to be successful with beginning phonics, which promptly leads to a discussion of oral language.

Oral Language

All aspects of reading are dependent upon oral language, and this includes decoding. Of obvious importance for the latter is the decoder's listening/speaking vocabulary. In fact, as was quoted in the previous chapter, "If the word that is unfamiliar in printed form is also unfamiliar in spoken form the reader who can sound it out will not understand the word any better than the reader who cannot sound it" (Brown, 1958, p. 69). Children who have serious mispronunciation habits also are likely to have problems with phonics. Here I refer to those who habitually use such pronunciations as "piture" for *picture*, "dis" for *this*, "childern" for *children*, and so on.

That these dependent connections do exist is the reason constant and continuing help with oral language is so important for success in phonics.

Visual Discrimination Ability

Since reading is a visual task, phonics also deals with the visual, specifically, with letters (graphemes) and their sequences in words. The ability to distinguish among letters is therefore another requirement for success with beginning phonics.

Most children seem to have little difficulty seeing that one letter is different from or exactly like another. When there are shortcomings, instructional time needs to be given to letter discrimination tasks (e.g., "Is this letter just like that one?") as a way of preparing for phonics.

Often, assigning names to letters can go right along with seeing which are the same and which are different. I mention this because a child's knowledge of at least some letter names is a decided advantage when it comes to starting phonics. Obviously, for example, it is much easier when a teacher can refer to letters by name ("j") rather than by description ("fish hook"). In addition, knowing their names is evidence of the ability to discriminate among them.

Auditory Discrimination Ability

Because the very nature of phonics is to deal with letter-sound relationships, ability to perceive both similarities and differences in speech sounds (phonemes) is also of basic importance.

It is customary for phonics instruction to begin with attention to the initial sounds in words; consequently an understanding that words comprise multiple blended sounds is another prior requirement. Added to that is the need to be able to hear as a distinct sound whatever happens to be the initial sound.[1]

At the start, instruction need only focus on sounds of spoken words. Soon, though, connections between sounds and the way they are represented in writing become a central concern of phonics instruction.

[1] What can be done to help children hear individual speech sounds is dealt with in the next chapter in the section entitled "Auditory Discrimination." Help with visual discrimination is included, too.

Knowledgeable, Competent Teacher

Thus far this discussion of what are being called contributors to success in phonics has focused only on the children. Yet, what any given child is likely to learn is very much dependent upon the knowledge and competence of his teacher. That she must be thoroughly knowledgeable about what can be taught is the reason the previous chapter detailed the content of phonics. To help her learn how to communicate that content to children is the reason for this present one.

To get started with that goal, the following section singles out some of the factors to consider when questions arise about a sequence for teaching phonics.

SEQUENCE OF INSTRUCTION

Admittedly, it is not common for teachers to devise their own phonics program, including the order in which its various components will be introduced. Nonetheless, it still is important for them to know what ought to be considered in choosing a sequence; otherwise they will have less understanding than they should of the reasons why certain children have certain problems.

Possible choices for instruction are made from the content of phonics, which, as the previous chapter pointed out, deals with syllabication, stress, and the sounds letters record. Since it is best to start phonics with single syllable words, attention to syllabication and stress is unnecessary at the beginning. Initial instruction therefore begins with attention to some letter-sound relationships.

Letters are divided into consonants and vowels, and, further, into categories of single letters and digraphs. Because it is easier for a decoder to deal with the sounds of single letters, attention should go to them initially. In addition, because consonant letters are more consistent in what they record, the attention should focus on some single consonants before any of the very important vowel letters and vowel sounds are discussed.

When sounds that are represented by consonant letters do get attention, it is important to remember that confusion might result when similar sounds are taught in too close succession. This means that teachers need to keep in mind the categories of "voiced" and "voiceless" sounds (see pages 11–12) and avoid teaching pairs like /b/ and /p/, /d/ and /t/, /g/ and /k/, and /s/ and /z/ one after the other.

Because of their basic importance, vowel sounds must be studied as soon as possible. Since so many children find it especially difficult to perceive and remember the short sounds, teachers should be ready to provide extra amounts of practice with them.[2]

Once the ten long and short sounds are learned and children are thus aware that a letter like *a* commonly records sounds called "long" and "short," they are ready—in fact *need* to learn when each sound is likely to occur in unfamiliar written words. This is when it is timely to teach generalizations like: When there is one vowel and it is not the final letter, it usually stands for its short sound. Because skill in phonics requires more than the ability to count vowels, these same children soon need to learn that what follows that single vowel also has relevance for pronunciation. And so it becomes time to highlight such generalizations as the one suggesting that vowels followed by *r* stand for special sounds.

Later, when multisyllabic words become common in written material, the need arises to help children understand what a syllable is and, secondly, what its significance is for decoding. This, of course, is the time to begin teaching generalizations pertaining to syllabication and, later, to stress. Meanwhile, letter-sound relationships are not forgotten, for instruction now centers on selected digraphs and also on the less frequently occurring single letters.

Phonics instruction thus progresses by moving from what is less difficult to what is more difficult; from what will be immediately useful to what becomes useful; and from what is known to what is as yet unknown.

INSTRUCTION

Having covered in this quick and general way some of the considerations that go into decisions about sequence, it is time to deal with the specifics of instruction. Although each thing that is taught should be used for decoding as quickly as possible, the specifics of instruction will be dealt with by giving separate attention to (a) teaching content, and (b) teaching its use. In no way, however, is the separate treatment meant to imply that all the essential content is taught first, then its use. Rather, the separate consideration is simply a convenient way to deal with two different but closely connected concerns.

Teaching Content

Whether the focus of instruction is on letter-sound relationships, on factors that affect those relationships, on syllabication, or on stress, two

---

[2] Interesting ways to help children remember letter-sound associations are described in Chapter 5.

kinds of teaching procedures are possible. One is referred to as *inductive* instruction; the other as *deductive*. Using letter-sound relationships as the instructional goal, let me explain what these terms mean.

Inductive Instruction. Dictionary definitions of "induction" offer such explanations as, "reasoning from particular facts to a conclusion about them." Applied to teaching letter-sound relationships, an inductive procedure would start with carefully chosen words ("facts") that exemplify whatever relationship ("conclusion") is to get attention. For instance, if a teacher wants to instruct children about the relationship existing between /s/ and s, written words beginning with s would be selected. Possibilities follow:

see	sign	snow
some	sun	sky
sat (or)	snake (or)	sailor
	seal	scissors
	star	
	scout	

Three groups of selections have been listed to show that inductive instruction can be initiated in more than one way. If children are able to read such words as *see, some,* and *sat,* these words could serve as illustrations of what is to be taught. If, however, no appropriate words are known by the children, a teacher might choose to begin with a bulletin board display of labeled pictures showing objects whose spoken and written names begin with /s/ and s, respectively. Once the pictures have been identified and discussed, label names can be transferred to a chalkboard, resulting in a list similar to the second one shown above.

Another teacher might choose to proceed differently. In this case, she initiates instruction by calling the children's attention to three words that have been discussed and displayed (*Sunday, Saturday, September*); in particular, to the fact that all begin with the same letter and sound. This teacher then asks the children to try to think of other words that begin the way *Sunday, Saturday,* and *September* start. Four possible responses have been listed as they might be given by the children, beginning with *snow.*

Ideally, of course, words used to illustrate letter-sound (grapheme-phoneme) relationships would be in the children's reading vocabulary, but that will not always be possible. One guideline that ought to be adhered to, however, is related to the fact that initial sounds in words generally are the easiest to hear as distinct sounds. This is why each illustrative list comprises words that begin with s and /s/. Ideally, all the words would have been single syllable words—again as a way of making it easier for the children to attend to the initial sound. As a way of making that sound maximally distinctive, each would also have started with an s followed by a vowel.[3]

Regardless of how words are chosen for inductive instruction, similar questions would be asked about them in order to teach the selected letter-sound relationship. To illustrate, let's say a teacher is instructing children who can read see, sat, and some; consequently those words would be written and the children asked to read them.

see
sat
some

Because phonics deals with both the visual and the auditory features of words, a teacher's first question might be, "Who sees something that's the same about the beginning of all these words?" (The three words were written on the chalkboard in the fashion shown above to highlight the initial s in all of them.) Once the identical visual feature is identified, the next question must deal with the auditory. Thus, a subsequent request to the children might be: "Would you read these words again and, as you do, see if you can hear something at the beginning that's the same in all of them.[4] . . . What sound did you hear at the beginning of all these words when you read them aloud? . . . Yes, that's a sound that s stands for. Now, when you see a word that begins with s you'll know the sound it probably starts with. (As soon as possible the children will also be learning that words which begin with sh start with a different

---

[3] This is an appropriate time to refer to a complaint of the linguist-critic; for he charges that phonics instructors erroneously act as if speech sounds are totally new to children when, in fact, they have been using them from the time they uttered their first word (Seymour, 1969). In response I would like to point out that phonics deals with familiar speech sounds in new ways. For example, the idea that a familiar word like "see" has a beginning sound is new to children. That this sound can be represented in written language by the letter s also is new.

[4] If the words were not in the children's reading vocabulary, the teacher herself would do the reading. In this case her request might be, "As I read these words, see if you hear a sound that's the same at the beginning of each."

sound.) Can you think of some words right now that start with the sound of *s*? I'll write them up here with *see, sat,* and *some* . . . ."

To give still more meaning to inductive teaching, let me now present an example that centers on another type of phonics content; namely, a generalization dealing with a group of sounds represented by vowels: When there is one vowel in a word and it is the final letter, it usually stands for its long sound. This instruction would not take place until the children know both the long and short sounds.

To help teach the generalization inductively, a teacher might list words like the following, each in the children's reading vocabulary:

we

no

she

go

hi[5]

To help the children induce the generalization from the five examples listed, a teacher would again ask questions pertaining to certain visual and auditory details: "How many vowels do you see in *we*? . . . Which of its sounds does the *e* stand for in 'we'?" After asking the same two questions about the remaining words, the teacher would then focus on the placement of the single vowel in each of the five words. This could be done with a question like, "Where is the one vowel in all of these words?"

To bring the relevant details together, the teacher continues: "You've told me three things that are the same about all these words. You said they have one vowel, the vowel is at the end, and it stands for its long sound. Noticing all those things about other written words will help you figure out what they say. Now, whenever you see a word you can't read and it has one vowel letter that is at the end, you'll know that vowel will have its long sound—or at least most of the time it will stand for its long sound. I'm going to write all those things on the board to help you remember them." As the teacher writes she reads:

---

[5] A list of words containing all five vowels would be preferable; however, suitable one-syllable words ending with *a* and *u* are non-existent.

1. one vowel letter
2. at the end
3. long sound

Pointing to each detail, the teacher next helps the children put into words the generalization getting attention. As soon as possible, they will also be helped to use it in decoding unfamiliar written words like *be* and, later, like *silo*.

Before discussing what might be called the "pros" and "cons" of inductive instruction, let me first present examples of deductive teaching. In that way the two can later be compared and evaluated together.

Deductive Instruction. Essentially, deductive instruction is a telling rather than a reasoning process. This does not mean, however, that it bypasses careful explanations. Let me demonstrate this with a description of a lesson, again having to do with the identification of the sound that *s* stands for in words like *see*, *sat*, and *some*.

As is true of inductive instruction, illustrative words in a deductive lesson need not be words the children can read. In fact, examples of appropriate words can be collected in any of the three ways described earlier, when inductive teaching was the concern. For our purposes now, let's assume the children being instructed can read *see*, *sat*, and *some*; and that their teacher has decided to use the words as a starting point in her lesson. She begins by writing them on the chalkboard:

see
sat
some

After the children read the three words, she would call their attention to the fact that all begin with the same letter, with *s*. Next she would point out that they begin not only with the same letter but also with the same sound. At this point the three words probably would be re-read, either by the teacher or by the children, with the request to listen for the initial sound in each. Next the teacher might choose to identify /s/ explicitly by saying something like, "The sound you hear at the beginning of all these words is something like what you hear when air is coming out of a balloon. It's the sound /s/. It's the sound *s* stands for in words like *see, sat,* and *some.*"

It is possible, of course, that the same teacher might bypass an explicit and isolated identification of /s/ and simply comment, after the words have been read aloud and the children asked to listen for the sound at the beginning, "That sound you heard at the beginning of these words is the sound *s* stands for." To see whether the sound really was heard by the children, she might next ask, "Can you think of some other words that begin with the sound you hear at the beginning of 'see,' 'sat,' 'some'? I'll write them if you can." Soon the board shows:

see soap
sat   Saturday[6]
some Sunday
    six
    seven
    seventeen
    seat

After listing responses on the board, this teacher might choose to reinforce the children's perception of /s/ by concluding: "To make sure you hear the sound that *s* stands for in all these words, I'm going to read both lists. If you can read the word, say it with me. If not, just listen as I read so that you can hear the sound that *s* stands for in all these words."

To explain still further the meaning of "deductive" applied to phonics, let me describe another lesson. This one deals with syllabication and is being carried on with children who are more advanced in reading. Like the first deductive lesson, it will be characterized by telling rather than by reasoning.

Being taught deductively is the generalization: When there are two consonants preceded and followed by vowels, there usually is a syllabic division between the consonants. To get started, the following words—all familiar to the children—are written on the board by the teacher:

---

[6] Responses like this provide an opportunity to point out that lowercase *s* and capital *S* stand for the same sound.

pencil
number
garden
picnic
accent

After the children identify the words, they might be asked to read them again and to listen for the number of syllables in each. Once it is agreed that all are two-syllable words, the next request is, "Can you tell me where these words divide?" Since the children know the words, they have no trouble responding. With their responses, a new list can be written in either of the ways shown below:

pen cil	pen	cil
num ber	num	ber
gar den	gar	den
pic nic	pic	nic
ac cent	ac	cent

    With unknown written words, visual cues must be used to help with syllabication. Consequently the teacher's next comments will deal with them. In deductive instruction she might say to the children: "I want you to notice something about all these words because it will help you figure out words you can't read. Notice, first of all, that the first syllable in each ends with a consonant and the second syllable in each begins with a consonant. But, that's not enough to notice. Let me point out something else. In all these words a vowel (pointing to *e* in *pencil*, *u* in *number*, etc.) comes before the first of the two consonants (pointing to the *n* in *pencil*, etc.). And there's one more thing to notice. In all these words the second of the two consonants that we've been talking about (pointing to the *c* in *pencil*, etc.) is followed by a vowel (pointing to the *i* in *pencil*, etc.). I've asked you to look for lots of things in these words, haven't I? Let's see if I can put all this together now, and then we can see how it will help divide words you can't read. I've said that if there are two consonants in a word that are preceded and followed by vowels, there usually is a syllabic break between those consonants. Now let me show you how this will help with words you can't read." Another list is then written:

ginger
condemn
pretzel
scarlet
perfect

"Can anyone read any of these words? [7]. . . Even though you can't, I bet you can tell me where they would divide into syllables. Later I'll read them and you can see if you were right. Remember, now, I've just been saying that when a word has two consonants that are preceded and followed by vowels, there usually is a syllable break between the consonants. Where do you think the first word up here divides into syllables? . . . That's right, between the n and the g, consonants that are preceded and followed by vowels . . . ."

Eventually the board shows:

gin ger
con demn
pret zel
scar let
per fect

[7] Using unfamiliar words at this point in the instruction is important because if the children could read the illustrative examples, a teacher would have no way of knowing whether they were using what they hear or what they see in responding to a question like, "Where does this word divide into syllables?" With unknown written words, the children have to rely on visual cues (two consonants preceded and followed by vowels) in order to respond, which is exactly what is required for decoding.

The teacher continues: "Now that we've divided these words into syllables, let me tell you what they say and you'll see that in every case you picked out the right place to divide them . . . ."

Which to Use? Now that examples of both inductive and deductive teaching have been given, the question of which to use needs to be considered.

The first thing to point out is that such a question does not require an either-or response. That is, teachers do not have to choose one procedure *or* the other. In fact, in the day-by-day work of the classroom, moving back and forth between the two probably is the most natural and, in the long run, the most productive way to proceed. Nonetheless, each does have some distinct advantages that ought to be kept in mind. For example, inductive instruction can provide children with a strategy for learning. It does this by getting them to look at written words in ways that can help them induce phonic generalizations not yet formally taught. It thus gives them an opportunity not only to be independent learners but also to experience what might be called the delight of discovery. Of course, not all of this will happen with all children; still, inductive instruction does have this very important potential. Used with beginners in phonics, it can also pave the way for a better understanding of what is being done when deductive methods are selected later on.

Were a teacher to use nothing but inductive teaching, serious drawbacks would result. In particular, it would slow down instruction to the point that a wide gap would soon exist between what children are learning and what they would find useful when they read. Therefore, and for the sake of efficiency, some instruction needs to be the deductive kind. In the long run, how well individual children learn from each method must always be the decisive factor when teachers make day-by-day decisions about the way a certain piece of phonics content will be taught.

When content deals with letter-sound relationships, it should also be the children who help a teacher decide whether to isolate sounds from words, and this should be so whether the teaching is inductive or deductive. Specifically, the position taken in this book is as follows:

1. Sounds can be isolated or explicitly identified whenever this seems to be required by particular children.
2. When consonant sounds are isolated from words, they are much more distorted than are the vowel sounds. Consequently teachers need to be especially careful when they attempt to pronounce them. This means they must avoid such unnecessary distortions as "suh" for /s/. It also means they must avoid such blatantly incorrect pronunciations as "er" for /r/ and "ul" for /l/.

3. Although consonant sounds—in spite of distortions—will sometimes have to be isolated from words when the connection between them and certain letters is first taught, they never have to be isolated when they are being used to decode unknown words. Why this is so will be clarified next as instruction in the use of phonics content is discussed; in particular, when the more advanced use is explained.

Teaching Use of Content

Whether an inductive or deductive method is chosen to teach phonics content, children should learn as quickly as possible about the usefulness of that content in figuring out unfamiliar written words. This means that all phonics instruction goes back and forth between teaching content and teaching its use.

Initial Use. Actually, use can be demonstrated much sooner than many teachers seem to realize. For instance, when beginners in reading know only a few letter-sound relationships, use can go along with whole word methodology. More specifically, if the children need to learn to read *book*, it need not be immediately identified for them. Instead, a teacher might proceed by writing some words on the board, all unfamiliar to the children:

took

walk

book

Teacher comments might begin with: "I don't think you can read any of these words but I'm sure you'll be able to tell me which one says 'book.' Listen to the beginning sound in 'book.' . . . Which letter stands for that sound? . . . Good. Now, what is the only word up here that could be 'book'?"

Later Use. When children are able to read a word like *book* and also know the sound that *t* stands for, another kind of use can be initiated. With this it would be appropriate to begin by writing and identifying *book*, and by reviewing the relationship between *t* and /t/. To help with the latter, known words beginning with *t* might be written and identified. Then the following words would be written in a way that highlights the similarity as well as the single difference:

book
took

After having the children re-read *book*, the teacher should comment about the close similarity between *book* and the unfamiliar word written beneath it. She might then mention that the second word sounds very much like "book" except that it begins with the sound of *t*. Naturally, the next question would be, "Can anyone tell me what this second word is?" If someone can, the first of what will be many uses of phonic substitutions has been demonstrated. If nobody can, the teacher will offer further help. For instance, she might choose to use the following:

book
took   I <u>took</u> the toy home with me.

In this case all the words in the sentence are known, with the exception of *took*. Now the teacher's question is, "What word would make sense in this sentence? What did you do with the toy? Remember, the word sounds like 'book' except it begins with the sound of *t*."

In those rare instances when even this amount of help is inadequate, the teacher would simply answer her own question. ("This word is 'took'. Notice how much it sounds like 'book'. 'Book', 'took'.") At this early point in phonics instruction, answering one's own questions is fairly common but is also very helpful in explaining their meaning.

To both specify and summarize other common uses of phonics content, the following lists should be adequate.

SUBSTITUTIONS: INITIAL SOUNDS

Known word	book	it	got
Known sound	/t/	/ă/ [8]	/sh/
Decoded word	took	at	shot

[8] In these listings, phonic [/ă/] rather than linguistic [/æ/] symbols are used to indicate the phoneme.

SUBSTITUTIONS: MEDIAL SOUNDS

Known word	act	man	get
Known sound	/n/	/ĕ/	/ŏ/
Decoded word	ant	men	got

SUBSTITUTIONS: FINAL SOUNDS

Known word	meat	he	ran
Known sound	/n/	/ī/	/sh/
Decoded word	mean	hi	rash

ADDITIONS: INITIAL SOUNDS

Known word	in	and	ink
Known sound	/p/	/st/	/br/
Decoded word	pin	stand	brink

ADDITIONS: FINAL SOUNDS

Known word	car	in	fir
Known sound	/d/	/ch/	/st/
Decoded word	card	inch	first

What could be called "subtractions" are not very common; still, they are useful in moving from such words as *star* to *tar* and *ran* to *an*.

More Advanced Use. Thus far in the discussion of the use of phonics content, only letter-sound relationships have been mentioned. That is, examples of decoding presented up to now have only shown how children can be taught to figure out new words (*took*) by using known words (*book*) and letter-sound associations (*t* = /t/). This type of decoding ability will not always be sufficient, however, simply because words that could offer help might not be known. This is why children eventually need to be taught how to use other phonics content for decoding.

Let me describe this more advanced decoding by describing the thoughts of a child who has been taught how to use content that deals not only with letter-sound relationships but also with syllabication, factors which affect sounds, and stress. To be maximally instructive, the thoughts as described here will be much more detailed than would ordinarily be the case.

For illustrative purposes let's say *hush* is the only word in the sentence shown below which this child cannot read. Let's also assume that helpful words (e.g., *crush*) are not known either and so an independent kind of decoding is required.

A hush came over the boys.

To decode *hush* the child's thoughts might proceed as follows: "This has only one vowel letter so I don't have to worry about syllables. It could only be a one-syllable word because every syllable has to have a vowel sound. Let's see. I know the sound that *h* usually stands for. I remember learning about it in first grade with words like *he* and *have*. Now for the *u*. That's a vowel and it's the only vowel and doesn't come at the end, so it probably stands for its short sound. Oh, oh, *s* and *h* together. Together they probably stand for the sound they record in words like *she* and *show*. Well, that takes care of all the sounds in this word. Let's see what happens when I put them together. Since the first sound is a consonant I'll start blending with the vowel sound." At this point the child's subsequent thoughts can be most graphically described as follows: ŭ→hŭ→hŭsh. Continuing, his final thoughts might be: "Oh, sure. Hush. The boys stopped talking."

Using all of this child's thoughts, let me now pinpoint the steps followed in this type of decoding.

The decoder's first concern was for syllabication. This is required by the fact that decoding deals with syllables, not words. As it happened, *hush* was only one syllable and so the whole of it could be dealt with immediately.

The decoder's second concern was for the sounds *h* and *u* and *s* and *h* were likely to record. Special attention had to go to *u* because vowel letters vary in what they represent. In dealing with *u*, the decoder correctly took into consideration all relevant visual cues: one vowel in a closed syllable and not followed by any of the letters that affect the sound it will represent. Correctly, too, the decoder did not look at *s* and *h* separately but, instead, dealt with them as one of the special consonant digraphs.

This careful consideration of letter-sound relationships was followed by blending. Having been taught that consonant sounds are particularly distorted when isolated from words, the decoder began with the vowel sound (ŭ) to which he then added the initial sound (hŭ). From that point on, blending proceeded in the more orthodox left-to-right fashion. (Had the unknown word started with a vowel, only the left-to-right direction would have been used: ă→ăc→ăct.)

Once sounds were blended, the decoder quickly recognized a word that was familiar in its spoken form. The context (sentence) in which *hush* appeared then verified the correctness of the decoding because it makes sense to say, "A hush came over the boys." Since the decoded word turned out to be one that was familiar in its spoken form, a decision about stress was unnecessary. Even if this had not been so, the fact that it was only one syllable ruled out the need for a decision.

In outline, then, the steps used to decode *hush* dealt with:

1. syllabication
2. letter-sound relationships
3. blending

Following similar steps, let me next demonstrate how written words of more than one syllable can be figured out. Once more I'll use the thoughts of a decoder, this time as he deals with *typhoon*, which he finds in the following sentence:

The storm turned into a typhoon.

The child's thoughts might proceed as follows. "Lots of letters in this word! In this case *y* would act like a vowel because if it started a syllable the *t* would be left alone and a syllable can't have just a consonant. *Ph* is one of those special digraphs, so there's probably a syllable break between the *y* and *p* because when a consonant (*ph*) is preceded and followed by vowels (*y*, *o*) there's usually a syllable division between it and the preceding vowel. Let's see now, that leaves *ty* and *phoon*. That double-*o* probably records one vowel sound. In that case this word would just have the two syllables. I'll take them one at a time beginning with the first. I know the sound of *t*, and the *y* probably stands for the long sound of *i* because it's recording the final sound in an open syllable. Now, let me put those sounds together: y($\bar{\text{i}}$)→ty. That takes care of that syllable. Now for *phoon*. *Ph* probably stands for the *f* sound. Together, *oo* has a long and short sound. I'll try the long one first because that's more common. I know the sound of *n*. I learned that a long time ago when I was learning words like *not* and *no*. Let me put those sounds together: $\bar{oo}$→ph$\bar{oo}$→ph$\bar{oo}$n. *Ty* and *phoon*. Oh sure, typhoon! I remember seeing a movie about a typhoon. They're really bad storms."

Like the decoder who successfully dealt with *hush*, this one followed certain steps. Again, his initial consideration was for the syllabication of *typhoon*. To reach the conclusion that it was two syllables, he made use of two generalizations:

1. When a consonant is preceded and followed by vowels, there often is a syllable division between the first vowel and the consonant. (In the case of *typhoon*, *y* was treated as a vowel and *ph* was treated as if it were a single consonant.)

2. Every syllable has a vowel sound. (This generalization was used twice. It helped the decoder decide that *y* was functioning as a vowel, and then it helped him conclude that *typhoon* had two but no more than two syllables.)

Once the two syllables in *typhoon* were identified with the help of visual cues, the decoder turned to letter-sound relationships. Although the description of his thoughts showed him giving separate attention to *t* and *y* when he dealt with the first syllable, he might also have used an initial consonant substitution; for instance, something like: *by→ty*.

In dealing with the second syllable, *phoon*, the long sound for *oo* was tried first because it occurs more frequently. Verification of its correctness came when the child recognized *typhoon* as a word he knew in its spoken form. In this way, both *typhoon* and *hush* demonstrate the close connection between oral language and decoding. For teachers, they also show the importance of putting words-to-be-decoded into a context (sentence) because that is what allows the decoder to conclude his efforts with the very important question, "Does this make sense?"

Although neither *hush* nor *typhoon* required attention to structural analysis, that often enters into the type of decoding now being discussed. In fact, it can enter immediately because affixes and inflectional endings usually are syllables. Let me illustrate this priority of word structure with still another example of another decoder's thoughts. In this case he is puzzling over *untie* when he finds it in the following sentence:

The man cannot untie the rope.

Having been taught about affixes and inflectional endings, this decoder looks at the *un* and decides it might be a prefix and thus a separate syllable. (Since the context indicates the unfamiliar word is a verb, the possibility that *un* is a prefix is great.) Mentally, this decoder lays *un* aside, knowing that it will be pronounced "ŭn" and that it will mean either "not" or "to do the opposite." (When prefixes like *un* are taught, learners should end up knowing both their pronunciations and the effect they have on the meaning of the root.) Having laid *un* aside, the decoder is now ready to deal with what he believes to be a root (*tie*).

At this point, different decoders are likely to follow different paths. One might immediately recall the connection between *tie* and a word he is able to read—*die*. Combined with a knowledge of the sound that *t* stands for, *die* enables him to use a quick initial consonant substitution: *die→tie*.

Another decoder might not be so lucky and has to go through a more detailed analysis, which would start with a consideration of the syllabication of *tie*. In this case the likelihood that *e* is silent suggests *tie* is a one-syllable root.[9] Thus, the decoder can immediately begin to consider letter-sound relationships. He recalls the sound associated with *t* and the generalization used for syllabication suggests the likely sound for *i*. The decoder is now ready to blend sounds, beginning with the vowel: i̶e̶→ti̶e̶. "Oh sure," he thinks "untie. That man couldn't loosen the rope."

Before proceeding to other features of advanced decoding ability, let me first summarize the points teachers ought to remember from the various descriptions of decoders' thoughts:

1. Although known words (e.g., *see, some, sat*) should be selected for teaching the content of phonics, unknown words (e.g., *hush, typhoon*) should be chosen when children are getting practice using that content. Were known words chosen for the latter, the decoding would be too artificial to provide maximum learning.
2. When children are decoding, unknown words ought to be put into the context of at least a sentence. This gives the children a chance to evaluate the correctness of their efforts by asking, "Does this make sense?" (What to do when the decoded word does not make sense will be discussed shortly.)
3. Attention to syllabication starts the decoding process. This means that children should be taught to scan an unfamiliar word for any visual cues that suggest it might be a derived or inflected word. If structural analysis has been taught well, they will be knowledgeable about the pronunciation of affixes and inflections and will also be aware of the effect they have on roots.
4. Once tentative decisions are made about the structure of an unfamiliar word, attention goes to the root, which is decoded syllable by syllable.
5. In decoding a syllable, children need to give special attention to letters that tend to vary in what they record. In scanning a syllable, they must also be encouraged to consider not letters in isolation but, instead, sequences of letters.
6. Once tentative conclusions have been reached about the likely sounds constituting a syllable, they have to be synthesized or blended. If the initial sound in the syllable is a vowel, blending proceeds in a left-to-right direction. If, to the contrary, the first

[9] This decoder might also have been taught that the spelling pattern c-v-e suggests a long vowel sound. In either case the conclusion about *tie* being a single syllable word is the same because it is based on the need for every syllable to have a vowel sound.

sound is a consonant, blending begins with the first vowel sound, to which that initial consonant sound is then added. (Such a sequence eliminates the need to pronounce consonant sounds in isolation.) From that point on, blending follows the order of the letters. To specify further these comments about blending sequences, additional examples are given below:

Word Being Decoded	Blending Sequence
aid	āi̵→āi̵d
urn	ur→urn
ilk	ĭ→ĭl→ĭlk
rust	ŭ→rŭ→rŭs→rŭst
guard	ar→guar→guard
shape	ā→shā→shāpé

7. Outlining steps for blending is not meant to communicate the notion that every child must be required to use all of them all the time. To the contrary, for there always will be individuals who can leap (ŭ→rŭst) rather than step; and that should be their prerogative. On the other hand, there also will be children who almost require half-steps and it is their right to have teachers who can provide them with both knowledgeable and carefully paced instruction.

Importance of Flexibility in Use of Content

Listing steps to be followed in more advanced decoding can be helpful but also misleading, because the sequence it points to is not always the one that ought to be used with every word. For instance, a somewhat detailed list of steps would show this sequence:

Concern	Focus
Syllabication	Word
Letter-sound relationships	Syllables
Blending	Syllables
Stress	Word
Does this make sense?	Word and context

Although the above sequence is helpful as a general guideline, it does not indicate the kind of thinking characterizing the most successful and efficient decoders. For instance, if an unfamiliar word happened to be something like *spiral*, an advanced decoder would be likely to have almost simultaneous thoughts about (a) this word being a two-syllable root; (b) the first of the syllables receiving the stress; and (c) the likelihood of *a* in the second syllable recording the *schwa* sound. Such thinking is logical because all three conclusions are connected. All three are also correct and useful, even though they are the result of a sequence that did not follow exactly what is noted in the list of steps presented above. What this suggests is that academic discussions of decoding can be less than totally successful in communicating the flexibility that is so important.

One further example of flexibility must be discussed before this chapter comes to an end. In this case it is a way of dealing with the fact that the letters we refer to as vowels vary in the sounds they record. This flexibility requires quick recall of the vowel sounds in our language, all of which are heard in the following words in which they are represented by the underlined letters:

VOWEL SOUNDS

Long Sounds	Short Sounds	Diphthongs	Other Sounds
ate [10]	add	oil	ooze
eat	end	owl	book
ice	if		law
ode	odd		
use	up		

Having available a mental listing like this one allows a child to deal flexibly and thus successfully with vowel sounds, the ones most likely to cause problems for decoders. To explain this flexibility, let me use a word that has already been decoded and discussed, namely, *hush*.

In the earlier discussion *hush* was systematically figured out, sound by sound. For the present discussion let's say that the decoder upon seeing *hush* immediately notices the visual similarity between it and a written word he knows—*push*. Let's also say he then uses an initial consonant substitution (/h/ for /p/), but this results in a word that does not make sense. In fact, it doesn't even result in a word. Knowing that another strategy must now be used, the decoder has some alternatives. He can systematically analyze *hush*, which is what was described earlier, or he can assume that the likely problem is with the sound recorded by the vowel. In this case he can mentally run through the inventory of existing vowel sounds, trying out each one in succession. With *hush* he can

[10] In a word like *ate* it would also be correct to underline both the *a* and the *e* because the pattern v-c-e suggests the long *a* sound for *ate*.

stop when he tries out the short *u* sound because this produces a word that does make sense within the context of, "A hush came over the boys."

Let me describe still another use of an inventory of vowel sounds, now with the word *shoes*. It appears in the sentence, "The man had on black shoes."

The first source of help with *shoes* comes from the context, which suggests it is likely to be some type of clothing. The spelling also suggests it is probably plural. With some decoders, this much help plus awareness of the sound *sh* stands for would be enough to indicate what the word is. Other decoders, however, might need additional help. They might have to recall related words they know—for instance, *toes*. Or, some decoders might have to rely on the more methodical letter-by-letter, sound-by-sound type of analysis. In either case they would come out with the sound "shows," something that does not make sense in the context of, "The man had on black shoes." Once more it is appropriate for the decoder to assume the problem might lie with the vowel sound and to try out fourteen other possibilities for *oe*. As it happens, what does produce a word that makes sense is the vowel sound heard in *ooze*. As it happens, too, flexibility again is a requirement for successful decoding and thus an important goal in phonics instruction.

DEALING WITH UNFAMILIAR WORDS

The only reason for teaching phonics is to help children become independent in dealing with unfamiliar written words. In fact, independent and successful decoding ability is the criterion that should always be used whenever efforts are made to evaluate one kind of instruction as opposed to some other kind.

While children are growing in their ability to cope with written words on their own, some will have to be identified for them. Consequently, my concluding remarks in this chapter will deal with a question that all reading teachers must consider, "What should I do with new words?"

When reading instruction is still in its beginning stages, many new words will have to be identified for the children; that is, whole word methodology will have to be employed.[11] Even when ability is more advanced, however, certain circumstances still will suggest the wisdom of offering total help. It might happen, for example, that a child is reading something aloud to others and comes across a word he does not know or cannot recall. Rather than have him "sound it out" in front of

---

[11] How to make whole word methodology maximally successful has been treated in detail elsewhere (Durkin, 1972).

his audience, the teacher might simply tell him what it is so that the flow of communication is not interrupted.

On most other occasions, words should be identified for children only (a) when their spellings are so irregular as to make even the most sophisticated decoding ability non-productive, and (b) when they are regularly spelled but require decoding ability that is beyond what the children can manage. Thus, in considering any new word, a teacher's thoughts must deal with the nature of the word itself; specifically, with the relation between the way it is spelled and the way it is pronounced. In addition, she must also be aware of what the children know and can do and, in the light of those considerations, decide whether to tell them what the word is or let them figure it out on their own. Remember, not to let children do the figuring whenever this is possible is to deny them an opportunity to grow in a very necessary requirement for successful reading: independence in decoding unfamiliar words.

All of the present chapter has been concerned with this goal of independence. Reaching it requires not only excellent instruction but also interesting practice for the children. The next and final chapter, therefore, describes some of the things that can be done to make phonics practice both interesting and productive.

Chapter 5   📖   📖   📖   📖   📖   📖   📖   📖   📖

PRACTICE

If children are to become proficient decoders, they must have repeated opportunities to learn and use the knowledge and abilities that go into decoding. In other words, they have to have practice. What might be called the raw bones of phonics practice is hardly appealing. This is why teachers need to work at adorning it in ways that will make it attractive, thus winning the children's attention.

The purpose of this final chapter is to help with the job of assembling interesting kinds of practice. Because one suggestion commonly prompts at least one more, the prediction is that by the end of the chapter you will have many more ideas for practice than have actually been described.

Ideas are grouped according to the goal they are designed to reach. This parallels teaching in the sense that instruction in phonics should also begin with the selection of a goal; that is, of something that needs to be taught, re-taught, reviewed, or whatever. Once such a decision is made, it is then time to consider a means for achieving the goal.

As possible means are described in this chapter, comments about them will be added from time to time. This is to ensure that the chapter ends up being more than a series of recipes; that, in fact, it becomes something that contributes to your understanding of what constitutes good practice—whether for phonics or something else.

The first kinds of practice to be described deal with letter discrimination and letter naming; consequently they come under the goal of visual discrimination.

VISUAL DISCRIMINATION

Most children do not have too much trouble seeing that one letter is like or different from another. Usually, too, letter discrimination tasks (e.g., "Is this letter exactly like that one?" or "Look at this letter and then draw a line under all the other letters that are the same.") can soon be combined with letter-naming instruction. In both, more attention should go to lower-case than to capital letters because the former will be used more frequently in reading instruction.

Once children have had the chance to learn some letter names, practice (repeated letter naming) is necessary to make the learning permanent. Just how much practice will be required varies from child to child and from letter to letter. What does not vary, however, is the need to make the practice as appealing as possible. With letter names this might be accomplished simply by using a hand puppet as a pointer. Descriptions of still other ways to add interest follow. For each, the underlying assumption is that practice is carried on only with children who need it. Otherwise even the most interesting ideas end up being little more than busy work.

When children are still at the level of matching rather than naming letters, procedures like the following can be helpful in providing necessary practice.

Teacher's job
    Purchase or make a cardboard rack containing 20 or more small pockets. Place a letter card in each, face down. (Use two cards for each of ten selected letters.)

Children's job
    Select one letter card, then another. If the two match, the cards can be kept. If not, they are returned to the pockets and another child makes other selections.

Teacher's job
    Draw vertical and horizontal lines on a ditto master to form rows of squares. In each square print a letter. Put small letter cards into envelopes. Give each child a sheet with the squares and letters, and one envelope.

Children's job
    Cover each square with a matching letter card.

To maintain interest, a slight variation of the above can be used; it will be enough to make the children think they are doing something different.

Teacher's job
   On a ditto master draw an umbrella similar to the one shown below.

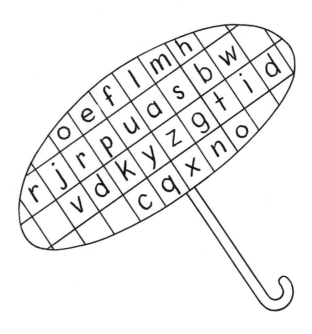

   Distribute a copy to each child as well as an envelope containing small letter cards.

Children's job
   Cover each letter on the umbrella with a matching letter card.

   Once children are adept at matching single letters, both the squares and the umbrella (or whatever is used) can be altered to show pairs of letters. This kind of matching should be done as quickly as children are able to deal with more than one letter, because it is like the visual discrimination involved in learning to read words.

   With the single letters, the squares and umbrella will become useful again after children have learned the names of letters. Now, instead of having the children match letters, the teacher (or a knowledgeable child) names a letter, after which the children cover it with a paper square.

Holidays often provide ideas fo· practice, including some for letter naming. What might be done as Halloween approaches is described next.

Teacher's job
Cut out small baby ghosts from white construction paper. Print a letter on each using both lower-case and capital forms. Place them in a grocery bag, now a "trick or treat" bag.

Children's job
Take turns pulling out ghosts and naming letters. Correctly named ghosts are kept, temporarily.[1]

Generally it is a good idea to end an activity with what might be called summary practice. This could be achieved with the suggestion just described by thumbtacking the ghosts to a bulletin board, after which all their letters would be named by the children.

Use of another holiday is in the next suggestion.

Teacher's job
Cut out egg-shaped pieces of construction paper, on which letters will be printed.

Children's job
Make Easter baskets and handles out of construction paper. Take turns naming egg-letters held up by the teacher. Correctly named eggs are put into baskets, to be taken home just before the start of the Easter vacation.

Reminders to teachers about using the above procedure have general relevance for practice; consequently they are detailed below:

1. Appealing activities can be used to create interest in less appealing ones. With the eggs and Easter basket, for example, unadorned letter-naming practice can come first, now described as a means for making sure lots of eggs end up in the baskets.
2. Letters should always be large enough to be easily seen. They should also be printed on light-colored paper, again to make sure that all are clearly visible.
3. Whenever taking turns is part of an activity, the instructional group should be sufficiently small that the children's patience is not taxed and interest is maintained.
4. Concern for academic achievement should never overshadow concern for the human factor. In the case of the baskets, for instance,

---

[1] Getting to keep things, even temporarily, is very appealing to children. Expect them to count what they have been able to keep to find out who has the most.

by the time practice comes to an end and they are about to be taken home, a teacher should have seen to it that no child is left with a too-empty basket.

5. Among primary-grade children, especially girls, activities like the egg-naming one often are doubly useful because of the likelihood that they will be played with at home.

For visual discrimination as well as all the other goals that are related to decoding ability, bulletin board displays can be productive. When each is being used for the first time, teacher participation generally is required. Most can eventually be used by the children alone, however. No display, by the way, should be considered a do-not-touch decoration. In fact, all the bulletin boards to be described in this and subsequent sections of the chapter are presented as instructional materials, the ones below as other materials for letter-naming practice.

Teacher's job

Close to the Christmas holidays, cut out small rectangular pieces of green construction paper on which letters will be printed. Prepare the background for a holiday bulletin board, leaving space for a Christmas tree, which will be assembled by thumbtacking the rectangles in increasingly shorter rows to form a large triangle (tree).

Children's job

Help construct a Christmas tree by correctly naming letters on rectangles. As each is correctly identified by individual children, that rectangle will be added to a quickly growing paper tree.

A different kind of tree figures in the next display.

Teacher's job

Cut out a large paper tree and thumbtack it to a bulletin board. On circular pieces of red construction paper (apples), print letters.

Children's job

Make the tree bear fruit by correctly naming letters shown on the apples, which will then be attached to the tree. At another time, pick apples from the tree by re-identifying letters.

Each month of the school year offers ideas for displays. The following would be appropriate for April:

Teacher's job

Prepare a bulletin board featuring a large paper umbrella. Cut out paper raindrops; on each, the capital and lower-case form of a letter will be printed. Give special attention to both forms of one letter each day during April so that before the month ends all the letters will have been reviewed.

Children's job
Each day identify the letters on a raindrop, which is then thumbtacked to the April bulletin board. Each day, too, name the letters already on the board.

Stories read to or by the children often suggest content for displays. For example:

Teacher's job
Once *Jack and the Beanstalk* has been read, prepare a bulletin board that has, first of all, a tall thick stalk made by rolling up green paper. Long leaves, cut from more green paper and displaying letters, can be attached.

Children's job
Take turns trying to climb the stalk by naming letters shown on the leaves. Misnamed letters mean a fall and an opportunity for someone else to attempt the climb.

An activity as ordinary as hanging up clothes could be highlighted in a display:

Teacher's job
Cut out two long and narrow pieces of paper, now considered poles for a clothes line. After attaching them at either end of a board, hang a piece of string between them to serve as the clothesline. Next, cut out pieces of paper in the shape of children's clothes and print a letter on each.

Children's job
Hang up clothes by correctly identifying the letters printed on them. When "dry," clothes can be taken down by re-naming the letters.

If hanging up clothes is viewed as a feminine task, another display could be selected to appeal to boys in need of letter-identification practice. For example:

Teacher's job
Cut out construction paper to look like the outline of an airport building; and, next, to look like clouds. Attach the building to the bottom of a board and the clouds at the top. Print letters on the clouds.

Children's job
Holding a small wooden or paper airplane, fly up to the clouds to

identify letters. A misnamed letter brings the plane crashing to the ground and gives another child the chance to be a pilot.

Let me conclude these descriptions of letter-matching and letter-naming practice with a few comments about the way both suggestions and materials can often be used in more than one way.

Multi-use is possible, first of all, when the goal of practice remains unchanged. When it is concerned with letter naming, rectangles for a Christmas tree—to cite one illustration—can later be described as bricks for constructing a building on a bulletin board.

Multi-use of materials also is possible when goals change. In fact, almost all the ideas described for letter-naming practice can be used later on when letter-sound relationships are the concern. For the latter, the job for the children would be to consider a given letter and to name words that begin (end) with the sound it records.

Should word-identification practice be the selected goal, suggestions for letter matching and letter naming become useful once more. Now, letters printed on materials would be replaced with words or, in some cases, with short phrases and sentences.

AUDITORY DISCRIMINATION

Just as it is necessary for children to be able to distinguish among letters, so too is it essential that they can make distinctions among speech sounds. In fact, it is the combination of the two abilities that allows attention to letter-sound relationships and then to decoding.

First, however, auditory discrimination must get attention to make sure that children do hear both differences and similarities in sounds. To help, suggestions for practice will be described in this section. The underlying assumption of all of them is that the children are aware that words comprise more than one sound; that, in fact, they can have beginning, middle, and final sounds. Assumed, too, is that instruction with auditory discrimination has already taken place and that there is the need now for practice. At this point, no assumption is made about the children knowing that speech sounds are recorded with letters. Instead, the focus is only on the auditory feature of words.

It should be noted, first of all, that special preparations are not always required for auditory discrimination practice. At dismissal time a teacher might simply comment, "If your last name begins with the sound you hear at the beginning of 'Monday', you can get your coat." Or, if large pictures are available that show multiple subjects, they can be used. With a large and colorful picture of a farm, a teacher's question might be, "Who sees something in this picture whose name begins with the same sound as 'boy'?"

Other practice requiring some preparation also makes use of pictures for auditory discrimination; for example:

Teacher's job
Draw a large wheel on a master ditto. In between the spokes draw eight simple pictures, four of whose names begin with the same sound.

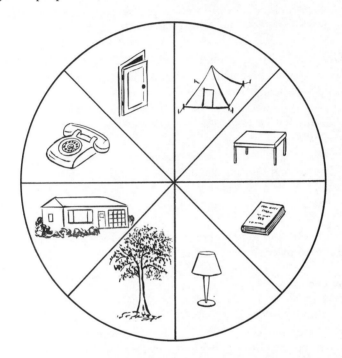

Distribute copies to the children and elicit from them the names of the pictures.

Children's job
Think of the names of all the pictures. Color the four whose names begin with the same sound.

Teacher's job
Distribute small pictures of objects to the individuals in an instructional group.

Children's job
Put into a pile pictures showing objects whose names begin with the same sound.

The picture cards mentioned in the practice just described can be used in a number of different ways. A teacher might hold all of them, allowing individuals to select one. If a child is able to name the selected picture and then a word that begins with the same sound, he gets to keep the card. Or, the cards might be distributed to the children, who then place them in boxes to which pictures have been pasted. In this case the job is to match initial picture-card sounds with the initial sound of the picture attached to a box.

Regardless of how teachers decide to use pictures for auditory discrimination practice, two guidelines need to be followed:

1. Unlabeled pictures should be used. (With labels, a teacher would have no way of knowing whether the appearance or the sound of a word was being used by children to respond to questions and requests. When auditory discrimination ability is the concern, it is the sounds that ought to be used; therefore labels should not be available.)
2. Teachers should always know the name a child assigns to a picture. (One showing an envelope might be called "envelope," but also "mail" or "letter.") Not to know a child's choice is to be unaware of the sound he is considering.

When auditory discrimination is the goal, small objects and trinkets can be used in place of pictures. For instance:

Teacher's job
Collect small objects and trinkets and place them in a large grocery bag, now a "grab bag."
Children's job
Select an object from the bag and name it. Then name any word that begins with the same sound.

Teacher's job
Collect additional objects and trinkets, placing all on a table. Have the children name them.
Children's job
Select any of the trinkets, then select another whose name begins with the same sound. Name the two.

With both the trinkets and the pictures, questions and requests as described in the suggestions only dealt with initial sounds. All, however, could be altered to focus on final sounds, and some could be used with medial sounds.

One word about final sounds; in particular, about the use of rhyming words to deal with them. Although I am aware that most commercial materials give considerable attention to rhyme as they concentrate on final sounds, I am also aware through classroom visits that when this is the case children commonly equate "words that rhyme" with "words that end with the same sound." As a result, they have been heard to conclude that words like "pet" and "met" end with the same sound but words like "pet" and "put" do not. The suggestion of this book, therefore, is to let children enjoy rhyme in poetry and songs but to omit it from instruction and practice that deal with auditory discrimination, at least until the meaning of "same last sound" has been firmly established. Some other observations about auditory discrimination practice follow.

1. When a child is unable to respond to requests like, "Name a word that starts with the sound you hear at the beginning of 'book'," at least three explanations are possible. First, he might not be able to perceive similarities and differences in speech sounds. Or, second, he might not yet understand the meaning of the request itself. When either or both of these explanations is correct, a solution lies in continued practice of a similar kind, but one in which the teacher will often respond to her own questions and requests. By doing so, she demonstrates their meaning and also contributes many examples of both similar and dissimilar sounds. With this type of continued practice, the two deficiencies can be remedied. The third possible explanation is totally different, thus requiring a different remedy. In this case failure to respond reflects the child's inability to recall appropriate words. Whenever poor memory might be the problem, riddles are helpful; for instance, "I'm thinking of a word that begins with the sound you hear at the beginning of 'book.' It's the name of something that flies." When wrong responses continue to be given (airplane), the two explanations referred to earlier are likely to be the correct ones.

2. When auditory discrimination practice does not use written language (e.g., "Who can think of a word that begins with the sound you hear at the beginning of 'sun'?"), certain responses are acceptable that would not be so were written language also being used. More specifically, should a child offer "Cynthia" as a word that starts with the sound heard at the beginning of "sun," it is correct because at that point only speech sounds are the concern. However, as soon as instruction and practice shift to letter-sound relationships (s stands for/s/), a response like "Cynthia" is no longer acceptable. Since it does begin with the right sound, it

should never be rejected without an explanation. Instead, it ought to be written on the board with a comment about the fact that the sound heard at the beginning is the one heard in "sun" but it is not spelled with *s* as is the case in *sun*.

Typically, as children are acquiring skill in auditory discrimination, they also are learning to read some words through whole-word methodology. When this is the case, known words can be used in practice that begins the shift from auditory discrimination to instruction with letter-sound relationships. Exemplifying the transition is the teacher who writes a word the children can identify (*rain*), asks them to read it, and then asks them to think of and name other words that start with the sound they hear at the beginning of "rain." Writing responses on the board gives this teacher the chance to mention that all the words begin with the sound heard at the beginning of "rain" and, secondly, that all start with the same letter. Reading *rain* plus all the other words now on the chalkboard also gives her the opportunity to demonstrate once more the meaning of "begin with the same sound."

To provide for the kind of auditory discrimination practice that combines known words and attention to sounds, games are often useful. Two possibilities will be described:

Teacher's job
On small cards print words the children can read. As in a card game, distribute them to a small group of children in need of auditory discrimination practice.

Children's job
The first player reads one of the words on the cards he is holding but does not show it to anyone.[2] If the child to his left has a word that begins (ends) with the same sound, he reads it and gives it to the first player. If not, the first player lays down his card. Whoever is out of cards first is the winner.

Teacher's job
On small cards print familiar words with the c-v-c spelling pattern (e.g., *him, sat*). Place them face down in the slots of a cardboard rack.

Children's job
Take turns selecting a card. Read the word and then name any other word that has the same medial vowel sound. A correct answer allows a child to keep the card; otherwise it is returned to the slot. At the end, the one holding the most cards is the winner.

---

[2] Not showing it is important because in auditory discrimination practice attention should be focused on speech sounds, not on spellings.

Before concluding this section on auditory discrimination practice, it might be helpful to put its concern into the broader perspective of decoding. Within such a perspective, the ability to perceive both similar and dissimilar speech sounds is seen to be a means to an end, namely, proficiency in figuring out unknown words in print. The means-end relationship must always be kept in mind; otherwise it is all too easy to turn a means (auditory discrimination) into an end-in-itself. Perhaps this is what happened when, in days gone by, teachers had children listen to environmental sounds or, perhaps, to different notes on a piano, and claimed this was a way to prepare for phonics. Perhaps it is the same means-end confusion that still prompts some teachers to assign workbook pages that make no contribution to a child's decoding ability. Simply put, what all of these comments suggest is the unceasing need for teachers to get into the habit of asking themselves, "*Why* am I doing what I'm doing?"

LETTER-SOUND RELATIONSHIPS

In a previous chapter in which instruction was the concern and knowledge of letter-sound relationships was the goal, the relevance of visual discrimination for that instruction became clear as samples of teachers' questions were mentioned; for instance, "Who sees something that's the same at the beginning of all these words on the board?" Subsequent comments by teachers clarified the relevance of auditory discrimination: "Let's read all these words. As you say them, listen for the beginning sound in each one." Thus, ability in both visual and auditory discrimination is required before instruction in letter-sound relationships can get started.

Once that instruction is begun, there is the need to plan for practice in order to solidify relationships to the point that children automatically think of certain sounds when they see certain letters. To assist with the planning, this section will describe practice whose aim is to help children remember forever connections existing between the sounds of our language and the letters of our alphabet.[3]

Helpful again are bulletin board displays; suggestions for some follow:

Teacher's job
After instruction in the sound *w* records has been given, prepare a display with the title, "Web of Words." A large paper spider and a web made with yarn will be featured. Cards displaying words begin-

---

[3] Most of the suggestions made earlier for letter-naming activities can be adapted to provide practice with letter-sound relationships.

ning with *w* and /w/ need to be thumbtacked to various parts of the web.

Children's job
Snatch cards from the spider's web by correctly identifying the words printed on them. Once removed, all the words will be re-read.

As was mentioned before, practice materials usually are adaptable and the bulletin board just described is no exception. With letter-sound relationships still the goal, cards displaying letters whose sounds have been studied could be attached to the web. Now each card is snatched away from the spider by naming a word that begins (ends) with the sound its letter records.

After children have learned that *c* is sometimes used to stand for /k/, a bulletin board like the following becomes useful for practice:

Teacher's job
Prepare a display entitled "Captain's Club," which shows the wheel of a ship made of paper. Prepare cards on which words beginning with *c* and /k/ are printed.

Children's job
Membership in the Captain's Club is gained by correctly naming a word card, which is then attached to the board. Later, all the words on the board will be re-read.

Use of the captain's board assumes children can read the words on the cards. Should that not be so, small pictures of labeled objects whose names begin with c and /k/ could be used instead. Or, if the children know a few appropriate words, they could be used along with the pictures.

The two displays described thus far highlight initial sounds that are recorded with consonant letters. The next example shows how a bulletin board can provide for practice with medial sounds. Since the medial sounds of most syllables are vowels, they are featured.

Teacher's job

Prepare a display with the title "Oscar the Octopus." In this case a paper octopus is the special attraction. Distribute small picture cards to individual children, some of which show objects and actions whose names have the short sound of *o* as their medial sound—for instance, *clock, hop, doll, pot, blocks, mop.*

Children's job

Quietly think of the names of the cards, putting together those whose medial sound is the short sound of *o*. Take turns naming those cards, which, if correct, are thumbtacked to the bulletin board. A label will then be attached to each. Re-name all the cards and words now displayed.

These skimpy descriptions of how bulletin board displays can be used for practice could result in poor communication about teaching because of their failure to include the very details that often make the difference between successful and unsuccessful use. And here, of course, success or the lack of it refers to whether the goal of the display is realized. Thus, no matter how attractive or interesting, Oscar's board would be considered a success only if it reinforced the connection between *o* and what is referred to as its short sound and, secondly, led to improved perception of this sound in medial position. With the help of the Oscar board, let me now specify some of the important details that were not mentioned. Hopefully, they will help you learn to use all the practice described in this chapter in ways that will be maximally successful in achieving its goals.

Use of the Oscar board might begin with some attention to Oscar himself. Writing *Oscar* and *octopus* on a chalkboard would allow for attention to common beginnings, both visual and auditory. Next could come a review of the short sound of *o*; this might be accomplished with the teacher asking, "Can you think of some other words that begin with the sound you hear at the beginning of *Oscar* and *octopus*? If you can I'll write them on the board." Soon the board shows:

Oscar   October

octopus   on

olive

operation

Since the Oscar board is to help with the short *o* sound in medial position, attention goes to that next: "Sometimes that sound of *o*— remember, it's called the short sound—is in the middle of a word. Can anyone think of a word in which 'ŏ' is the middle sound?. . . Nobody? . . . I'll say one and then I bet you'll be able to think of some, too. Hot." Soon many examples are suggested, which, again, are written on the chalkboard.[4]

Now it is time to use the Oscar bulletin board in the way described earlier under "Teacher's job" and "Children's job." Let me add a few more comments, however, this time to explain why three procedures were used with the board.

Procedure	*Reason*
Used the names of pictures.	To make sure children were able to perceive the short *o* sound in medial position.
Added labels to the pictures.	To reinforce the connection between the short *o* sound and the letter *o*.
Had children read all the labeled pictures.	To provide for additional practice both in hearing the short *o* sound and in seeing that it often is recorded with *o*.

As was suggested with "Oscar the Octopus" and also with "Captain's Club," alliteration makes for useful titles when letter-sound relation-

---

[4] To review a point made earlier in the chapter: The concern is not only for a sound but also for the way it is usually recorded in written language. Consequently, if a child were to offer "palm," it could not be considered correct because in this case *a* records the sound getting attention. This should be explained to the children, because mere rejection benefits neither their learning nor their self-confidence.

ships are getting attention. This suggests other titles like "Bat the Ball," "Sing the Song," and "Catch the Cat."

At other times construction paper can be cut out to represent a large version of something familiar to the children, which is now to be used as the background for a display. For example, should there be the need to work on the connection between *h* and /h/, two very large paper hands could be cut out and used with a title like "Helping Hands." Outlines of such things as a telephone, mitten, umbrella, door, or igloo might also be used for other backgrounds at other times.

Still another possibility for a bulletin board is described below:

Teacher's job

Divide the board into separate sections. In each, display a letter or digraph, either consonants or vowels. Distribute unlabeled pictures of objects and actions whose names begin with the displayed letters and the sounds they usually record.

Children's job

Take turns naming the pictures. After naming one, tell what the first letter(s) of the name would be so that the teacher can attach the picture in the appropriate section of the board.

Like so many of the displays that have been described, the one above can eventually be used by children working alone. Now the picture cards would be placed in two or three cardboard boxes attached to the bottom of the bulletin board. Individual children could elect to place the pictures in the appropriate sections, perhaps at free-choice time, should that be part of a schedule.

One more possibility for a letter-sound bulletin board makes use of flowers:

Teacher's job

Cut out flowers, stems, and leaves. On the center of each flower print a single letter or digraph whose sound has been studied. Arrange the flowers on the board. Cut out a few paper bees, to be placed on the board too.

Children's job

Hold a paper bee and, like one, fly from flower to flower, naming a word that begins (ends) with the letter(s) appearing on their centers.

Less elaborate materials are equally helpful in establishing connections between letters and sounds. Something as ordinary as two plastic clothes baskets can be used in a way that will have special appeal for boys. In this case letter cards would be attached to the baskets for a game of phonics basketball. Participants, divided into two teams, would take turns listening to a word pronounced by the teacher and throwing the ball into the appropriate basket. Specifically, if the word was "Eskimo" and the baskets displayed cards showing in one case *a* and in the other *e*, the ball would have to be thrown into the latter to score a point.

Because of the special difficulty of distinguishing among and remembering vowel sounds, extra amounts of practice generally are a requirement. Whereas the basketball game gave attention to initial sounds, a simple card game like the following should help with medial sounds:

Teacher's job
Prepare a number of small letter cards showing: $\bar{a}$, $\breve{a}$, $\bar{e}$, $\breve{e}$, $\bar{\imath}$, $\breve{\imath}$, $\bar{o}$, $\breve{o}$, $\bar{u}$, $\breve{u}$. In random order distribute some to the children. The cards remaining are the deck.

Children's job
Listen to each word pronounced by the teacher (e.g., "with"), in particular to its medial sound. If holding the letter card that goes with that sound, show it. If correct, the card can be discarded; if wrong, another card has to be selected from the deck.[5] The first child out of cards is the winner.

For variation, words named by the teacher could be selected from a word-card deck. In this case, when a child displayed what he believed to be the correct letter card, he would be shown the word so that he himself could see whether his decision was correct.

The next game to be described demonstrates again that time-consuming preparations are not always necessary for effective practice:

Teacher's job
On the chalkboard list twenty letters and digraphs whose sounds have been studied.

Children's job
Write 1 to 10 in a vertical column on paper. After the numerals, write any ten letters or digraphs that appear in the chalkboard list. Next, listen as the teacher names a word. If its beginning (final) sound is spelled with a letter or digraph appearing on your page, circle it. In this game the first child to circle all of his letters is the winner.

When letter-sound relationships are the concern, art projects can help—although they should not be over-used for this purpose. To illustrate, after attention has been given to the sound *v* stands for, paper

---

[5] In games like this one, penalties encourage serious attention and discourage wild guessing.

vases filled with violets could be made by the children, perhaps as a gift for their mothers. Or, when they have learned about the sound associated with *l*, paper lollipops would be an appropriate project. Another activity, described below, should help children remember the sound to associate with *f*.

Teacher's job
Prepare a ditto master of simply-drawn objects whose names begin with *f* (e.g., feather, face, fire, flag, fence, fountain, foot). Distribute copies to the children. Elicit from them the names of the pictures. Write the names on the board, giving attention to the common visual-auditory feature.

Children's job
Make a fan by folding paper. Color and cut out the pictures. Paste them in the folds of the fan for decoration.

Art work used for phonics prompts repetition of a point highlighted before: Teachers must be careful to avoid turning means into ends-in-themselves. Such a reminder is necessary because with art projects, means-end confusion occurs very easily. To be specific, vases and violets designed to stress the connection between *v* and /v/ can end up being nothing more than a lovely vase with violets. Or, a fan originally chosen to give attention to the association between *f* and /f/ can end up being just an attractively decorated fan. To prevent this, teachers must be sure to add those details (*f* printed on the fans) and those explanations ("All these pictures begin with the same letter and sound that you find in *fan*. That's why they make a good decoration for the fan.") that make the difference between interesting art work and an interesting art-phonics activity.

What becomes apparent again in these comments is the basic importance of teachers' asking themselves, "*Why* am I doing this?" Answers will provide perspective and keep an activity on the right road, one leading directly to the goal for which it was originally selected.

PHONIC SUBSTITUTIONS AND ADDITIONS

As the earlier chapter on instruction pointed out, use of letter-sound associations for decoding begins with substitutions and additions. For example, the child who can read *red* and knows the sound associated with *f* is ready to learn how to use both to decode *fed*. Or, if he is familiar with a word like *in*, he is prepared to use that plus his knowledge of the sound of *f* to figure out the identity of *fin*.

Proficient use of known words and sounds for decoding also depends upon practice; consequently this section singles out activities aimed at that goal. Since it is common to teach consonant sounds prior to vowel sounds, initial examples will show the use of known words and consonant sounds.

An obvious and probably too-frequently-used possibility is to have children work with columns of words like the following:

cat	card	and	an
sat	cart	sand	and
fat	carp	band	ant
bat	Carl	hand	
mat		land	

The first two lists illustrate initial and final substitutions; the last two, initial and final additions. In each case, the first word and the sounds used to form the others are assumed to be known. What must also be assumed is that when instruction in the use of additions and substitutions is just beginning, a teacher will not only have to ask the questions ("What word would result if I changed the c in cat to an s?") but will also have to supply the answers ("It would say 'sat'."). Eventually, after practice has been provided, more and more of the answers will be coming from the children.[6]

A more interesting way to get answers is described next.

Teacher's job

To make a fishing pond, paint a cardboard box blue. For the fishing pole, attach a magnet to one end of a piece of string and a long, thin stick to the other. Next, on small, fish-shaped cards, print known words that can be used for phonic additions and substitutions. To each of these cards attach a paper clip. Put the fish into the pond. Make a set of letter cards.

Children's job

Using the magnetic fishing pole, take turns fishing for words. After naming whatever word is caught (*can*), try to respond to the teacher's question; for instance "What would that word be if it started with [teacher holds up *m*] this letter instead of *c*?"[7] A correct response allows a child to keep his fish. Otherwise it must be thrown back into the pond.

---

[6] Using the third column of words for practice in phonic additions requires that *and* be repeatedly identified: *and, sand; and, band;* etc. Otherwise the practice will be with phonic substitutions.

[7] If the group is still having difficulty with substitutions, the teacher could help by writing *man* on a nearby board.

As soon as it is appropriate to do so, the difficulty of the above procedure—or any like it—can be increased. Instead of beginning with a known word (*can*), an unknown one (*man*) would be selected. Now the task for the children is to identify the new word by recalling a related one (e.g., *can*) that is known. This is not only more difficult, it is also more realistic in that it duplicates what a child must be able to do when he is reading on his own and comes across a word he doesn't immediately recognize.

Currently, instructional materials are giving much attention to phonograms, which allow for practice in phonic additions. Using phonograms that have been studied, a teacher could type a ditto master to show something like the following:

f	*s*	*b*	*r*
__an	__un	__et	__ip
__ib	__and	__ut	__ock
__at	__at	__it	__ib
__un	__ock	__un	__ob

With the above, the assignment would be to write the letter indicated in the spaces and to decide what the resulting words are.

To change the practice into a game, a teacher could prepare a set of cards, each showing about six phonograms. One card might look like this:

```
┌─────────────────────────┐
│  __ap      __ick         │
│  __ell     __ile         │
│  __ug      __ing         │
└─────────────────────────┘
```

Each child playing the game receives a card. Participants then take turns selecting a small letter-card from a deck. If the letter chosen can form a word with one of the phonograms on that child's card and, secondly, if the child can say what the word is, he puts that letter in front of the phonogram. The first child to make six words on his card is the winner.

When instruction has dealt with phonograms, bulletin board displays can again be useful. Two possibilities will be described:

Teacher's job

Prepare a display to be called "Iceberg Hop." Cut out white construction paper to make icebergs, which will be attached to the bottom of the board. On the peaks, print phonograms that have been studied. Make a set of letter cards and a small paper penguin.

Children's job

Become a penguin by holding one. Then look at the letter card held by the teacher and recall the sound it records. Hop from iceberg to iceberg by naming the words that result when that letter and the phonograms shown on the icebergs are combined.

Teacher's job

Prepare a spring bulletin board that will feature three large daisies with petals that can be rotated. On the center of each daisy print a phonogram. (They can be changed periodically.) On the petals print consonants, either single letters or digraphs.

Children's job

Take turns spinning a daisy by rotating its petals. As this is done, name the words that are formed when the letter on the petal to the left of the flower's center is combined with the phonogram.

Whenever sounds are added (*an→can*) or substituted (*can→man*), there always is the possibility that unfamiliar words (*car→carp*) or even nonsense syllables (*car→dar*) will result. Should either be used, it often is asked, or should a deliberate effort be made to avoid both?

First, are nonsense syllables "permissible"? Those who stress that reading must always be "meaningful" often prohibit their use. However, when the reason for exercises like *car→dar* is kept in mind (to give children practice in substituting sounds), something like *car→dar* is meaningful and, if done successfully by a child, provides evidence of ability in making substitutions. It could even be argued that it is more reliable evidence than when the resulting sound is a real word. Nonetheless, nonsense words should not be allowed to constitute the bulk of practice activities, if only because they tend to be less interesting.

What about words whose meanings are unknown? Specifically, what about allowing for inclusion of a word like *carp* in practice with phonic additions and substitutions? What was said about nonsense syllables applies to words like *carp*, but in this case one further observation is called for. The occasional use of words whose meanings are unknown gives a teacher the chance to add to listening/speaking vocabularies. Too frequent use in phonics practice, however, would be burdensome and, again, unlikely to appeal to children.

Before concluding this section on phonic additions and substitutions, a few more examples of practice will be cited, beginning with some that focus on vowel sounds.

When children have learned to distinguish among and remember the short vowel sounds in medial position—this is very difficult for some—chalkboard practice is a possibility. In this case, individuals can be assigned space and asked to write as a start a familiar word like *cat*. Directly under it, related words named by the teacher would be written to provide practice in substituting sounds—in this case words like *cut* and *cot* would be appropriate. For similar practice, other word groups could include *rob, rub, rib; pan, pen, pin; hat, hot, hut;* and *big, bug, bag*.

After children know the short and the long sounds and, in addition, have learned a generalization that describes when each often occurs in words, they are ready for more writing and more practice in substituting sounds. In this case, the end-product would be two columns showing contrasting pairs of words. For example, beginning with *cap*, the word named next by the teacher would be *cape*. At the end, columns might show such pairs as these:

cap	cape
hat	hate
cut	cute
rob	robe
mad	made
rip	ripe
hid	hide
not	note

References to children writing at a chalkboard prompt a reminder, the need for which has been suggested in the course of visiting classrooms. Observed during those visits is that when children take turns writing something on the board, only the one doing the writing is interested. Consequently, the reminder to teachers is that the better procedure is to have a small group writing simultaneously.

One further kind of practice—the most advanced—cannot be neglected. It was first described in Chapter 4 when the thoughts of a decoder figuring out *hush* and *typhoon* were recorded (see pages 68–69). Much of this type of practice will be unadorned, but at this stage the satisfaction that comes from being successful can be just as much a source of motivation as are the penguin and the octopus and the bumblebee. At the start, though, a little embellishment is possible. For instance, using a string, to which small letter cards can be clipped, this more advanced addition of sounds can proceed in ways that are portrayed on page 98:

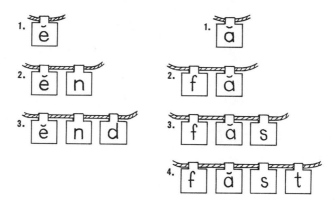

In this "bead stringing" practice, diacritical marks are necessary for dealing with the variability of vowels. Since in actual decoding it is the whole of a syllable that helps a child assign sounds to vowel letters, practice activities should duplicate reality as quickly as possible. To do this, unfamiliar words would be placed in sentences so that the decoder can use syntactic and semantic cues along with phonological cues. Use of the latter would follow the guidelines that were outlined earlier on pages 71–72. Proficiency in this type of decoding is the ultimate goal of phonics practice.

REFERENCES

Bloomfield, Leonard. "Linguistics and Reading." *Elementary English Review*, XIX (April–May 1942), 125–130, 183–186.

Bloomfield, L.; and Barnhart, C. L. *Let's Read*. Detroit: Wayne State University Press, 1961.

Brown, Roger. *Words and Things*. New York: The Free Press, 1958.

Carroll, John B. *Language and Thought*. Englewood Cliffs, New Jersey: Prentice-Hall, Inc., 1964.

Cordts, Anna D. *Phonics for the Reading Teacher*. New York: Holt, Rinehart and Winston, Inc., 1965.

Deighten, Lee C. *Vocabulary Development in the Classroom*. New York: Teachers College Press, 1959.

Durkin, Dolores. *Teaching Them to Read*. Boston: Allyn and Bacon, 1970.

———. *Teaching Young Children to Read*. Boston: Allyn and Bacon, 1972.

Fries, Charles C. *Linguistics and Reading*. New York: Holt, Rinehart and Winston, Inc., 1963.

Fries, Charles C.; Wilson, Rosemary G.; and Rudolph, Mildred K. *Merrill Linguistic Readers*. Columbus, Ohio: Charles E. Merrill Books, Inc., 1966.

Gleason, H. A. *Descriptive Linguistics* (Rev. Ed.). New York: Holt, Rinehart and Winston, 1961.

Hall, Robert A. *Sound and Spelling in English*. Philadelphia: Chilton Company, 1961.

Makita, Kiyoshi. "The Rarity of Reading Disability in Japanese Children." *American Journal of Orthopsychiatry*, XXXVIII (July 1968), 599–614.

Prator, Clifford H. *Manual of American English Pronunciation.* New York: Rinehart and Company, Inc., 1958.

Rasmussen, Donald; and Goldberg, Lynn. *SRA Basic Reading Series.* Chicago: Science Research Associates, Inc., 1970.

Seymour, Dorothy Z. "The Differences between Linguistics and Phonics." *The Reading Teacher,* XXIII (November 1969), 99–102.

Smith, Henry Lee. "A Review of *Let's Read.*" *Language,* XXXIX (January–March 1963), 67–78.

Smith, Henry Lee, *et al. The Linguistic Readers.* Evanston, Ill.: Harper and Row, Publishers, 1965.

Stott, D. H. Manual for "Programmed Reading Kits 1 and 2." Toronto, Canada: Gage Educational Publishing Limited, 1970.

Walden, James (ed.). *Oral Language and Reading.* Champaign, Ill.: National Council of Teachers of English, 1969.

Wardhaugh, Ronald. "Syl-lab-i-ca-tion." *Elementary English,* XLIII (November 1966), 785–788.

———. *Reading: A Linguistic Perspective.* New York: Harcourt, Brace and World, Inc., 1969.

Wylie, Richard E.; and Durrell, Donald D. "Teaching Words Through Phonograms." *Elementary English,* XLVII (October 1970), 787–791.